LOOKING BACK AT BRITAIN

PEACE
AND
PROSPERITY

1860s

PEACE AND PROSPERITY

1860s

Brian Moynahan

 Reader's Digest | gettyimages

CONTENTS

1860s IMAGE GALLERY

FRONT COVER: A family playing croquet – one of the few outdoor games imported into Britain and not invented – at the Gisburne Croquet Ground, Lancashire, in 1865.

BACK COVER: Colonel Gardiner, Commander of the Maharajah's troops in Kashmir, India, in an albumen print made in 1865.

TITLE PAGE: A little boy rides his rocking horse, with his big sister by his side, in 1861.

OPPOSITE: The village of Clovelly in Devon photographed in September 1860.

FOLLOWING PAGES:

Strand on the Green overlooking the River Thames between Chiswick and Kew, west of London.

Victorian holidaymakers strike a group pose on a rocky shore at the end of the decade.

The dining rooms at the London International Exhibition, South Kensington, 1862.

A group of fishermen near the Coldstream Bridge over the River Tweed on the England–Scotland border, 1862.

OUTWARD-LOOKING
NATION

The decade was still young when tragedy struck Queen Victoria. Her beloved Albert died and she retreated into mourning within the privacy of her family. In contrast, the British nation grew ever more expansive, its people travelling the world as traders, explorers, emigrants, colonists – above all, as rulers.

HOME FROM HOME Lieutenant Colonel William Ritherden with his daughter in Madras, trying out a new sewing machine in about 1865.

LOSING ALBERT

Late in November 1861, Prince Albert was drenched in a rainstorm. He caught a cold he could not shake off. Queen Victoria found his illness 'tiresome … I cannot tell you *what* a trial it is to me'. At the time she could not know, but her husband was in fact dying, in his prime at 41.

Albert had a final benefit to give to the country he had served quietly but well as Prince Consort. He made sure that Britain was not sucked into the American Civil War. The war had broken out in April that year. Britain was neutral, but many sympathised with the Confederates, particularly in Lancashire, where the textile factories were starved of cotton from the southern states. There was outrage when a Federal warship seized two Confederate envoys from a British ship as they sailed for London. Lord Palmerston, then Prime Minister, drafted a fierce ultimatum to Washington.

A copy was sent to the Queen. Albert read it. 'This means war!' he said, and dragged himself to his study to rewrite it, giving Washington the chance to save face by blaming an over-eager warship captain. 'I am so weak,' he said, 'I have hardly been able to hold the pen.' Washington duly backed down and released the envoys. It was the last thing Albert wrote. His physicians diagnosed 'gastric and bowel fever', the euphemism for typhoid fever. He died on December 14.

A nation in fine shape

The editorial in *The Times* two days later made an extraordinary claim, not so much about Albert, whom it praised fulsomely, but about the state of the nation. Britain, it said, had reached a 'degree of general contentment to which neither we nor any other nation we know of ever attained before'. It was a proud boast, and it smacked of the truth. By 1861, Britain was an historic phenomenon. The country accounted for less than 2 per cent of the population of the world, and just

A MAN WORTHY OF RESPECT
Prince Albert was in his prime when this photograph of him (right) was taken at the beginning of 1861. By the end of the year, he was dead. 'With Prince Albert we have buried our Sovereign', lamented Benjamin Disraeli, the future Prime Minister. 'This German prince has governed England for twenty-one years with a wisdom and energy such as none of our kings has ever shown.'

Albert was disliked as a German when he arrived in 1840 to marry Victoria, and he always remained an outsider. They spoke German in private – the Queen asked him for 'einem kuss' as he lay on his deathbed (below). Nonetheless, he was the driving political and cultural influence in what was still a working rather than ceremonial monarchy. The marriage was arranged, but it proved a love-match, real and lasting and stormy – 'Victoria is too hasty and passionate', he would say. Albert was painstaking, thorough and business-like in all he did. When he started a model dairy farm at Windsor, he made sure it made money. He had a shrewd and non-partisan eye for politics, but disliked London and its small talk. When he was gone, the Queen immured herself in grief.

MEMORIALS TO THE PRINCE CONSORT

The public, as if finally realising the worth of a man they had not appreciated when he was alive, gave the name Albert to pubs, boats, embankments, bridges, roads and squares up and down the land – and to tens of thousands of baby boys. Official monuments were begun almost immediately, like the Albert Memorial in Manchester (above), designed by Thomas Worthington with a sculpture of Albert by Matthew Noble, completed in 1867. A similar monument was raised opposite the Albert Hall in Kensington (right), itself an impressive reminder of the Prince's hard work on behalf of his adopted country. Ten years before his death, Albert's efforts in staging the Great Exhibition had led to a profit handsome enough to fund the Hall and the magnificent museums of South Kensington.

0.2 per cent of its land surface. Yet it was well on the way to acquiring the largest empire the world has ever known and would soon rule a quarter of humanity. Not only that. Britons clothed much of the world, in cottons and woollens, and supplied it with locomotives, shipping, coal, banking and insurance services, engineers, planters, miners, ships' crews, and – in North America and Australasia – with emigrants. The British accounted for a quarter of world trade.

The influence was exceptional, but so was the country. Visitors like the American poet and essayist Ralph Waldo Emerson found that 'the prestige of England' gave a confidence that the French or Belgians could not carry. 'An English lady on the Rhine,' he observed, hearing a German speaking of her party as foreigners, exclaimed, 'No, we are not foreigners, we are English, and it is you who are the foreigners ...'.

Its people might often be brutal, Emerson found, in love with boxing and public executions, and always ready 'for a set-to in the streets, delightful to the English of all classes'. But they had 'myriad personalities', which he attributed to the strength of the middle classes, 'always the source of letters and science'. They were also 'many-nationed: their colonisation annexes archipelagos and continents, and their speech seems destined to be the universal language of man.'

Fond remembrance

Of the many memorials to Albert, those that peppered London's Kensington reflected the new national grandeur. The Albert Hall, its vast roof a triumph of engineering, was intended originally as a 'Hall of Arts and Sciences', for conferences as well as concerts, complementing the great museums nearby, of Science and Natural History and arts and design in the Victoria and Albert.

Opposite the Albert Hall was the Albert Memorial, mooted as soon as he died and begun within two years, the competition to design it won by George Gilbert Scott, master architect of Victorian Gothic. Albert is the centrepiece of the shrine, surrounded by the emblems of the continents, each by a different sculptor – America, Africa, Asia and Europe, all profoundly affected by Britain, and in part peopled and ruled by British stock. An upper group of sculptures represents Manufacture, Agriculture, Commerce and Engineering, in much of which Britain led the world, redolent with steam hammer, blast furnace, engines and ships.

The Albert Hall, its vast roof a triumph of engineering, was originally intended as a 'Hall of Arts and Sciences'…

A podium frieze celebrated the arts, commemorating 169 poets, sculptors, painters, musicians and architects. At the time, writers of the utmost pedigree were entertaining Britain's newly literate masses. Thackeray's *The Virginians* was almost his last work, but Dickens was still at the height of his powers: *Great Expectations* was published in 1861 (the same year as Mrs Beeton's classic *Book of Household Management*). Lewis Carroll, pen name of Oxford mathematician Charles Dodgson, brought out *Alice in Wonderland* three years later. Wilkie Collins, an opium addict, was writing the first detective novels in English: *The Woman in White* appeared in 1860 and *The Moonstone* in 1868.

The Pre-Raphaelite Brotherhood, the association of artists including Holman Hunt, Millais and Rossetti, and devoted to recapturing the religious sincerity of pre-Renaissance painting, had disbanded a few years before, but it continued to influence men like William Morris. A poet, painter and craftsman, and a socialist thinker of note, Morris was devoted to the Gothic and the excellence of medieval arts and crafts. He revolutionised house decoration and furniture.

Only music in Britain lacked living artists of world class. That, George Bernard Shaw was to say, was because it lacked the support that the upper classes gave to 'racing, millinery, confectionary and, in a minor degree, to literature and painting'. Music was one of the rare areas where Victorians suffered from a feeling of inferiority. The Italians, Germans and Austrians were admired, but 'the British musician, let him be ever so talented, ranks scarcely above the ordinary artisan'. In the angles of the memorial's niches were what were held to be the typically British qualities of Fortitude, Prudence, Justice and Temperance.

Though 'Albertopolis', as some called it, was in Kensington, London did not dominate in the same way that France, say, was in thrall to Paris. The great provincial cities had an energy and pride quite distinct and independent from the capital. Albert Square in Manchester, with its own Albert Memorial, had a Town Hall as grandiose within as without, with a circular granite staircase, vaulted ceilings, and a Great Hall brilliant with 12 frescoes that took Ford Madox Brown 15 years to complete. The city itself – some called it 'Cottonopolis' – was a pulsating place, so Benjamin Disraeli said, of 'illumined factories with more windows than Italian palaces and smoking chimneys taller than Italian obelisks'.

Troubles abroad

Britain was politically and socially stable, a rarity in mid-19th-century Europe, where France had recently passed from Second Republic to Third Empire, Germany was yet to be united as a nation, Garibaldi was fighting a war of independence to liberate Italy from the Austrians and Rome from the Pope, and Russia had only just freed its serfs. In contrast, the 1860s were notably peaceful for the British. True, British cavalry under Lord Elgin burned the Chinese imperial Summer Palace in Peking (Beijing) in 1860. This act of wanton vandalism enabled Elgin – son of the man who had taken the Marbles from the ruins of the Parthenon – to settle the Opium Wars by forcing China to cede Kowloon as well as Hong Kong to Britain. In New Zealand, the Maoris were fighting the British settlers. But there was nothing going on to compare with the Crimean War or the Indian Mutiny of the previous decade.

On the Continent, Prussia was newly aggressive in the hands of Otto von Bismarck. The early summer of 1864 brought the first ominous rumble. At stake was the claim to the duchies of Schleswig-Holstein on the border between north Germany and Denmark. Lord Palmerston, an expert in foreign affairs as well as Prime Minister, said that only three people understood the Schleswig-Holstein question. One of them, Prince Albert, was dead. The second, a German professor 'is insane, and I, the third, have forgotten all about it'. Had the French and British taken a strong line, perhaps the crisis might have been averted. But they did nothing. Prussia defeated Denmark in two months and annexed the duchies.

Although they had enjoyed Austrian help against Denmark, two years later the Prussians turned on their erstwhile allies, attacking and humiliating Austria in the Seven Weeks' War. The way was now clear for Bismarck to create the North German Federation, essentially a united Germany, which went on, in 1870, to rout the French at Sedan in the Franco-Prussian War. Wilhelm I of Prussia was then proclaimed Emperor of Germany – ironically in Paris. The twin elements of German nationalism and Prussian militarism, now on the loose on the Continent,

FOR EMPIRE AND ADVANCEMENT
Among the British officers in China during the Second Opium War was Anglo-Irishman Garnet Wolseley (seated). The only way forward, he had once written, for an officer like himself who could not afford to buy a commission, was to put himself in extreme peril. He achieved this by getting severely wounded in the Crimean War. His conspicuous courage continued to such effect that by 1860, when this photograph was taken, he had risen from ensign to brevet lieutenant-colonel.

Wolseley's great hero was Charles Gordon, who was also fighting in China at the head of a private force, the Ever Victorious Army, paid for by the European merchants in Shanghai. Gordon smashed the Taiping rebels, earning himself the nickname 'Chinese' Gordon. He was killed in Khartoum in 1885, two days before a relief expedition under his old friend Garnet Wolseley arrived to rescue him.

SEA POWER
The Navy was the sinew of the expanding empire, enabling Britain to project its advanced technology around the globe. The officers of HMS *Encounter* (right), a venerable screw-steam sloop, played an important part in the Second Opium War with China, escorting two gunboats out from Portsmouth to the Far East, opening Chinese ports to British shipping and bombarding their forts. The *Encounter* had served earlier on the Russian Pacific coast, and would go on to Japan before returning to Portsmouth.

SERVING QUEEN AND COUNTRY

would have profound consequences. It needed foresight to spot it, but Albert, with his sophisticated political understanding, was no longer there. For the moment, though, Anglo-German relations seemed good enough.

WHIGS AND TORIES

Britain's monarchy combined well with developing parliamentary democracy. Two great parties, the Conservatives and Liberals, descendants of the 18th-century Tories and Whigs, dominated politics, with a continuity and tradition unknown outside the English-speaking world. In a broad sense the tradition of alternating between two parties, one centre-to-left, the other centre-to-right, remains to this day as an underlying identity of British politics. In Europe it might take riots or a revolution to force a change of government, but in Britain an election sufficed.

Despite its prodigious energy, the country was run by old men. Lord Palmerston, Liberal Prime Minister for the second time from 1859 to 1865, was known to have 'created Belgium, saved Portugal and Spain from absolutism, rescued Turkey from Russia, and the highway to India from France' – and that was said back in 1841, when he was merely in mid-career. Leo Tolstoy, the great Russian novelist, recollected a peasant dragging himself out of a bog to ask: 'Tell me, who is this man Palmerston?' That, Tolstoy said, was true fame.

The Liberal line-up
Palmerston was a 3rd Viscount. Lord John Russell, his foreign minister and successor, was the son of a Duke (the 6th, of Bedford) and had also cut his political teeth before the 1832 Reform Bill. William Gladstone, waiting in the Liberal wings, was in his fifties – as was Benjamin Disraeli on the Conservative side, shortly to finish his climb up 'the greasy pole' to succeed Lord Derby, another leader born the previous century.

Age and breeding meant that the era was stable and sensible, but it did not mean that it was prudish or dull. Far from it. Palmerston was tall, handsome and very fond of the ladies. He was nicknamed 'Lord Cupid' by those who liked him, 'the aged charlatan' by those who did not. Politicians were refreshingly robust in their descriptions of one another. Disraeli called Palmerston 'an old painted pantaloon, very deaf, very blind and with false teeth'. Palmerston was proud of his conquests, and, ever methodical and frank, recorded them together with his failures in his diaries. He had three children with his mistress, Emily Cowper, née Lamb, who co-existed with other mistresses from society and the *demimonde*. The couple eventually married. Palmerston was a wit – '*rien ne perce un habit rouge*', 'nothing gets through a redcoat', he said with sly reference to Waterloo when hunting in the rain with Napoleon III – and a big spender.

Lord John Russell was a tiny man, 5 feet 5 inches tall and weighing just 8 stone (50 kg). He was old enough to have visited another small and ferociously ambitious figure, Napoleon, during his exile on Elba in 1814. Despite being a member of one of the grandest Whig families in the land, Russell was not well provided for – ducal younger sons rarely were. As a young man, he had written a

A WELL-CONNECTED WOMAN
The Victorians were not as strait-laced as we imagine. This beauty, in a portrait painted by Sir Thomas Lawrence (a child prodigy with his own studio in Bath at the age of 12), was Emily Lamb, who became Countess Cowper when she married Earl Cowper. She also became the mistress of Lord Palmerston and gained a reputation as one of the 'most profligate women in London'. She was a famous hostess: though many deplored her morals, few declined her invitations.

Emily was the sister of Lord Melbourne – an earlier Liberal Prime Minister and political confidant of the Queen – whose wife was notorious for her passionate affair with Lord Byron. Emily's relationship with Palmerston began in about 1809. When her husband died, she allowed a short widowhood and then married her lover in 1839.

LORD PALMERSTON
Palmerston with his 'stepdaughter' Lady Jocelyn, who was Frances Cowper before her marriage. It is almost certain that Palmerston was her real father. He had two other children with Emily Cowper (above) before the couple married. He left his estates to one of them, William Francis Cowper-Temple, with the wish that he should assume the name and arms of Palmerston's family, the Temples. Palmerston continued to philander after his marriage to Emily. In 1863, then serving as Prime Minister and in his late seventies, he was cited as co-respondent in a divorce entailing a claim for £20,000 damages. The case was dismissed.

novel and a play – Disraeli said they were 'the feeblest in our literature' – as much to earn money as to express an artistic urge. Russell's house in Richmond was given to him by Queen Victoria, for he could not afford to buy his own.

Gladstone was the son of a wealthy Liverpool merchant, an Anglican with Nonconformist leanings. Unusually, he was conservative as a younger man and grew more radical as he aged. He attempted to save fallen women, seeking out prostitutes to speak to, and had an unconventional friendship with an ex-courtesan, Laura Thistlethwayte. He felled trees to keep fit, and he once walked 33 miles in the pouring rain to escape the Queen's estate at Balmoral. Victoria would have been happy to see him go.

The Conservative corner

On the Tory side, Lord Derby shared the public passion for horseracing – *noblesse oblige*, for the world's greatest race was named for a forebear. He was a regular at Epsom and Newmarket and a shrewd judge of horseflesh, adding to his already colossal fortune with winnings of £100,000 from the turf. Derby's natural successor was Disraeli, the most extraordinary of Europe's leading politicians. Born a Jew, usually a social and political liability in itself, Disraeli was not baptised an Anglican until he was 13. He was an adventurer and a dandy, with ruffled shirt, velvet trousers, loud waistcoats and hair in ringlets, who scorned bourgeois morality. 'To be a great lawyer', he said as a young man, 'I must give up my chance of being a great man.' He gave up law studies instead.

Disraeli speculated in South American mining stocks, writing pamphlets pushing the shares, and was all but ruined. He wrote a novel, *Vivian Grey*, about an ambitious, unscrupulous young man and his downfall. He published it anonymously, but the truth was soon out: the central figure was clearly a self-portrait. It did not help that the book sneered at figures in literary London who were almost as easily recognisable. He toured the Ottoman Empire, guided by an old servant of his hero, Byron, revelling in the exotic splendours of the Turkish court (and needing treatment for venereal disease on his return). He feared the 'cold, dull world' would ignore his 'strong necessity for fame'.

Disraeli went into politics for action – 'action may not always be happiness,' he wrote, 'but there is no happiness without action' – and the chance of getting 'power o'er the powerful'. Another attraction was that a parliamentary seat brought immunity from debt, for Disraeli was hounded by a queue of creditors. His maiden speech as an MP in 1836 was so over-ornate that it was all but drowned out by catcalls and laughter. But his last words were clear: 'Ay, and though I sit down now, the time will come when you will hear me.' His charm helped him carve out his career and entranced the Queen. 'Everyone likes flattery', he noted, 'and when it comes to royalty, you should lay it on with a trowel.'

Abundant talent

These were strikingly intelligent and well-read men. Gladstone read and spoke Latin, Greek, Italian, French and German fluently, got by in Spanish and had a little Norwegian. He was 'gallimaufrous', with a hotchpotch of interests. Palmerston had the same flair for languages. As a young boy, he had spent two years on the Grand Tour with his parents, and he was chosen to deliver orations

WILLIAM EWART GLADSTONE
In politics, as in much else, Gladstone was notably unconventional. He first entered Parliament as a Tory, in 1832, but he moved to the left over the years. He joined the Liberals in 1859, became leader in 1867 and subsequently was Liberal Prime Minister four times. He was a master of parliamentary debate, with a voracious appetite for work: at one point he was both Leader of the House and Chancellor of the Exchequer. Queen Victoria disliked him intensely, thinking him 'an old, wild and incomprehensible man' who spoke to her in private 'as if I were a public meeting'. Though a humane reformer in policy, this photograph, taken in about 1860, catches in his eyes and mouth a ruthlessness and severity of temperament glossed over in painted portraits.

continued on page 28

LORD DERBY

Seen here (left) in 1861, Lord Derby was three times Prime Minister and one of the grandest men alive. A 14th earl, his family were known as 'the kings of Lancashire' for their vast estates and fortune. He was fond of horseracing and was often seen at meetings amidst 'loose characters of every description … chaffing, rowing and shouting with laughter'. A classical scholar and orator of distinction, he was once offered – and declined – the throne of Greece.

BENJAMIN DISRAELI

Disraeli (below) was a phenomenon. The other leaders of the day were Etonians, Harrovians and Oxbridge men, from well-established or noble families. Disraeli was none of these. He was a writer of scandalous novels, an adventurer with a Jewish background. But he was also a brilliant orator, a charmer who won over the Queen, and a pragmatic 'One Nation' Tory who sensed that his party should cultivate working class support.

HIVE OF INDUSTRY

Britain was an industrial power of unequalled strength, the 'workshop of the world'. Fortunes were being made from iron and steelmaking, ship-building and ship-owning, mining, bridge-building, locomotive-making, cloth and cotton manufacture. Industry was well distributed around the country, with different regions specialising in different manufactures, but London – despite being better-known for dominating world finance and commerce – was still the greatest industrial city on Earth. Chemicals, photographic plates and cameras, ladies' fashions, shotguns, artillery shells, umbrellas, and the world's first iron battleship, HMS *Warrior*, were all made in the capital. This is the scene in 1867 in the engineering workshops of the Thames Iron Works, the major London shipbuilders.

MISTAKEN PROPHET
Karl Marx arrived in London with his family in 1849. Here he furthered his research into politics and economics in the reading room of the British Museum. He supported himself with sporadic journalism and help from his collaborator, Friedrich Engels, whose father had a cotton factory in Manchester. In 1867 Marx produced the first volume of *Das Kapital*, his magnum opus, in which he predicted the eventual triumph of socialism over capitalism, and the withering away of the state in a classless communist society. It made almost no impact in Britain: he sent a copy to Charles Darwin, which remained unread.

in Latin and English as a schoolboy at Harrow. Derby, for all his gambling, was a formidable scholar who wrote an original translation of the *Iliad*, and became Chancellor of Oxford. Only Disraeli excelled him as a debater and orator.

Solid social foundations enabled the country to cope with explosive growth in population and production. Karl Marx was living in Highgate – his collaborator Friedrich Engels was in Manchester – mapping a future dominated by class war in his *Das Kapital*. He sent a copy to Charles Darwin, believing himself to have discovered laws of history similar to Darwin's explanation of the laws of the natural world. Darwin did not get beyond the first page or two – Marxism never made much of an impression in Britain. Society avoided the worst stresses between

Marxism never made much of an impression in Britain.

proletariat and capitalist. The British had what Gladstone called 'a sneaking kindness for a lord'. The nobility were harmless, by and large, and had endearing eccentricities. They were sporting, they were to the fore in good works and, with notable exceptions, they were not disturbingly clever or gifted. They had good manners, and younger sons rubbed shoulders with commoners – at Westminster, in the army, the City and the colonies.

A balance between town and country, industry and land, underpinned mid-Victorian society and its prosperity. The market for British manufactures was growing at home and abroad, while foreign produce was still limited on the home market, wheat included. The countryside had 3.5 million acres under wheat, with crops running as high as 40 bushels an acre, and often over 30. The landed classes flourished, not through deference and the class system, but because they had land, and those broad acres – let to tenant farmers, sold off as building land for the new cities, or exploited for the coal beneath it – made them rich.

The pits were producing 60 million tons of coal a year, and the advent of wire rope and the rotary steam engine had freed women and children from coal haulage in modern pits. Chemical by-products of iron and coke underpinned a growing industry producing fertilisers, sulphuric acid, washing powder. New inventions – for example, in 1862 of 'linoleum', the application of linseed oil to floor coverings – spawned new factories. Cornwall was a world mining centre, not just of tin but also of copper – the Tamar valley was Europe's major source. At the peak, 650 beam engines were at work, pumping water from the mines.

A growing population

It was the swelling labour force that made this possible. The growth of population in Britain was extraordinary. So, darkly, was the stagnation in Ireland. In 1801, the population of the British Isles was 15.6 million. A little over half a million lived in Wales and 1.6 million in Scotland. England and Ireland were the giants, with 8.3 million and 5.2 million respectively. By 1861 the overall total had reached 27.8 million. Wales had passed the 1 million mark and Scotland 3 million. England had shot up to 18.8 million. Ireland, devastated by famine and emigration, had barely budged from 5 million: indeed, compared to its highest point of over 8 million in 1841, the population had collapsed.

A similar pattern continued in the 1860s. The total reached 31.3 million, with most of the growth in England – highest in the Northeast, London, the Northwest and West Midlands and lowest in the Southwest and East Anglia. The agricultural counties slid to 17 per cent of the population. Of the cities, only London and Glasgow exceeded the half million mark in the 1871 census. London was a colossus – called the 'Modern Babylon' by Disraeli, simply 'the Smoke' to its inhabitants. The city seemed larger than life itself, the seat of government and centre of arts and entertainment. Much of world trade was financed through the City, the world's largest money market, and shipped through its mighty docks. London was also the world's largest industrial city, with chemicals and printing works, gunsmiths and explosives makers, bell-founders, furniture-makers, tailors and dressmakers, brewers, jewellers, silversmiths and food processors.

The population of the capital reached 3 million by the end of the decade, with most of the increase due to incomers. The birthrate in London was well below the national average of 5.1 children per woman, on a par with rural Wales and the Isle of Wight, while Liverpool, Swansea and the northeast industrial belt around Newcastle were well above. Glasgow had hurtled from 77,000 in 1801 to 420,000 in 1861, then 522,000 by decade's end. Leeds leapt from 53,000 to 259,000, Manchester 75,000 to 351,000. Liverpool and Bristol, thriving ports in the 18th century, grew six-fold and three-fold respectively; Newcastle quadrupled.

Some towns were almost wholly new. The seaside resort of Brighton started the century with just 7000 residents, but was near 100,000 by 1871. Cardiff, under 2000 at the start of the century, ended it at 128,000. Railway towns like Swindon and Crewe were unrecognisable from the bucolic backwaters of pre-railway days. Swindon – a small Wiltshire town of barely a thousand souls before the Great Western Railway decided to locate itself there – had 14,000 people by

LOCAL TRANSPORT
Despite steam powering the railways, the workhorse was still more often than not a real creature of flesh and blood. This horse-drawn tram of 1864 ran on rails between Swansea and the Mumbles, a curious cross between stage coach, charabanc and railway train.

the end of the 1860s. Middlesbrough was rolling fields and barns until the directors of the Stockton and Darlington railway extended the line to make it easier to ship coal down the Tees. When Gladstone toured the north in 1862, he remarked of the Teesside town: 'This remarkable place, the youngest child of England's enterprise, is an infant, gentlemen, but it is an infant Hercules.'

Glaring exceptions to this population growth were the Scottish Highlands – land clearances restarted in the 1860s, as tenants were moved off to create 'deer forests', treeless shooting estates – and Ireland. The mass emigration that started with the Irish famine of the 1840s was still going on. In the 1860s some 850,000 left Ireland, some for Liverpool and England, but most for North America.

A NEW ERA OF TRAVEL

This was still a railway age, its prosperity and progress steam-driven. The length of track in Britain increased by almost half over the decade to 13,170 miles and the annual number of passengers virtually doubled to almost 300 million. Rail gave people of all classes unprecedented mobility. About one in ten travelled First Class, one in five Second, and the rest went 'Third and Parliamentarian'.

The original Third Class rail carriages were open to the weather, often had no benches to sit on, and were attached to slow-moving goods trains. The 1844 Railway Regulation Act, introduced by Gladstone, obliged the railway companies to offer third-class passengers at least one train a day that would travel at a minimum of 12 mph, with covered carriages and fares of not more than a penny a mile. The 'parliamentary carriages', named in Gladstone's honour, were no Pullmans. 'No night lamp, one door only on each side', a description ran, with 'no provision of air in bad weather, when doors and windows are closed'. The Midland line was best, the Great Western and the Eastern Counties vied for worst.

The Queen, naturally, fared rather better. The railway companies built special coaches for her in the same dark maroon as her horse-drawn carriages, with the royal emblem on the central panel and silver door handles. The interiors were lined with silk damask and crowns on the ceilings were surrounded by rose, shamrock and thistle 'carved and painted after nature'. The carpets were Axminster and the whole carriage was lined with Kamptulicon, a recently patented composite of cork and India rubber that reduced vibration.

Going abroad

It was increasingly by steamship that Britain exported its people as well as its manufactures. In tonnage terms, steamships were catching up with sail. In the 1840s there had been fewer than a thousand steamships, with a combined capacity of 123,000 tons, against a fleet of 23,500 sailing ships of 3 million tons. Sail was not yet done for – the incomparable tea clipper *Cutty Sark* was not launched until 1868 – but the yearly construction of steamships shot up over the decade from 72 to 280, with steam tonnage reaching 725,000 against sail's 4.5 million.

Many of Britain's emigrants went to Canada. The British North America Act of 1867 established a federal Dominion of Canada, encompassing Ontario,

TRAPPED IN GRIEF

THE QUEEN AND JOHN BROWN
After Albert's death, Queen Victoria
retreated into isolation and grief. Three
years later she was photographed at
Balmoral with two of her daughters,
Princesses Alice (standing) and Louise.
Albert's portrait dominates the scene like an
icon. Victoria still dressed in mourning
black, and her non-appearance was
resented by the public, who thought her
self-indulgent. The press said pointedly that
a private grief did not excuse anyone from
fulfilling public obligations.

Her Scots servant John Brown (above) –
a gillie at Balmoral, always known as
Johnny – was brought down to Osborne
House with her pony Lochnagar in the hope
that she would take more exercise. Brown
led the Queen's pony when she was out
riding, and slowly he helped her out of her
depression. He was devoted to Victoria and
she appreciated his devotion – 'discreet,
careful, intelligent, attentive,' she said,
'handy and willing to do everything'.
Rumours of an affair were rife. In July 1866
Punch printed a famous spoof 'Court
Circular' reporting that: 'Mr John Brown
walked on the Slopes. He subsequently
partook of a haggis. In the evening Mr John
Brown was pleased to listen to a bag-pipe.
Mr John Brown retired early.' In truth,
Brown gave the Queen companionship
and eased the ache of Albert's absence.
'His only object and interest is my service',
Victoria said. 'God knows, how I want so
much to be taken care of.'

Quebec, New Brunswick and Nova Scotia. Manitoba and the Northwest Territories were added in 1870, British Columbia the following year. 'Dominion' status meant that the country was self-governing in all but foreign affairs.

Convicts were still being transported to Australia, though this was becoming rare and the practice was formally abolished in 1868. Voluntary emigration to Australia, still divided into individual colonies, had been boosted mightily by the discovery of gold. The population of New South Wales and Victoria had shot up in a decade from 267,000 to 886,000 by 1860. Most of that vast land was still unexplored, and the 1860s saw pioneering expeditions by John McDouall Stuart, namesake of the Stuart Highway, and Robert O'Hara Burke and William Wills.

The importance of the navy

The key to Britain's empire was its navy, the largest in the world – the British were at pains to ensure it was at least as large as any combination of potential enemy ships. It enabled them, together with the equally prodigious merchant navy, to project their influence over thousands of miles to the two giants of the East: China and India. China, already forced to cede Hong Kong, was compelled in 1860 to open even more ports to British shipping. In India, rule passed from the East India Company to the Crown and the powers of the Raj were formalised.

> The key to Britain's empire was its navy, the largest in the world … at least as large as any combination of potential enemy ships.

In Africa, it was a time of exploration. David Livingstone's second great journey was laying the foundation for British colonies north of the Cape. John Speke and James Grant left England in 1860 on their expedition to confirm Lake Victoria as the source of the Nile. Samuel Baker with his wife Florence reached the inland sea that they named Lake Albert. Lagos was annexed in 1861, but in 1864 an expedition against the Ashanti on the Gold Coast was overwhelmed by malaria and incompetence. There was criticism of Britain's meddling in West Africa. Sir John Hay, an MP whose brother died in the Ashanti campaign, said that the government 'send other men to die with wonderful courage … of fever, of thirst, of want of shelter on the burning plains and fetid swamps of Western Africa.'

In some cases, London rid itself of unwanted territory. In 1852 the Colonial Office had acquired the Bay Islands off the coast of Central America, without telling the Foreign Office. Piqued, in 1861 the latter made a treaty transferring them to Honduras, without informing the Colonial Office. Lagos was seized largely because a Briton, John Beecroft, got into trouble with local rulers. Palmerston sent a note to the Kosoko of Lagos reminding him that his lands were 'near to the sea, and that on the sea are the ships and cannon of England'.

The government was keen to minimise the costs and administrative efforts involved in running an empire. It favoured self-rule wherever possible. Canada ran through money, particularly when extra troops were sent because of possible embroilment in the American Civil War. Dominion status was an attempt to get the place to pay for itself. Canada was reluctant to do so: it wanted the spirit of freedom, Gladstone complained, separated from the burdens of freedom. The constitutions that London authorised for the dominions were remarkably progressive – male suffrage, triennial parliaments – to encourage self-sufficiency. Such liberal largesse, in contrast, was notably lacking in India.

RULING THE WAVES
Royal Navy ironclads like this one (left), in 1867 caught midway between sail and steam, projected Britain's power around the world. Such was the navy's size and reach that a *Pax Britannica* was imposed on the world's sea lanes.

AT HOME ALL OVER THE WORLD

From the hill-town of Simla in northern India, declared the summer capital of the Raj in 1864, to equatorial Africa, British colonials had a genius for making themselves at home. They created a 'little bit of England' wherever they went.

COLONIAL GAMES
At an altitude of 2130m (6988ft) in the foothills of the Himalayas, Simla was cool compared to the fierce summer heat of Delhi and the plains. By 1865 it had acquired a cricket ground amid the forests of oak, pine and rhododendrons, to go with its churches, botanical gardens, zoo, boarding school, bandstands and other necessities of colonial life. Here (left), the Sunday Picnic Club is playing the modestly named World XI in front of the recently completed pavilion.

A few thousand miles away, the garden party below was played out in an African colony, probably at Government House in Lagos. The African and British dignitaries and their wives are dressed in equal Western finery – a little over-formal for a game of croquet, perhaps, but evidence of how fast fashion in dress as well as sport travelled around the empire. The All-England Croquet Club at Wimbledon was not founded until 1868, three years after this photograph was taken.

RAIL INDIA
Britain exported its railway expertise around the world. This station near Calcutta, photographed around 1867, bears the distinctive stamp of Victorian railway design. The railways became the backbone of British India. They propped up the status of the Raj as visible evidence of British industrial and technical skill. They tied the sprawling sub-continent together, and delivered its markets to British exporters. They were massive employers, in particular providing jobs for Anglo-Indians. And in the last resort, they had strategic value as a means of moving troops in the event of a further mutiny. They also, of course, helped to keep British locomotive and engineering works in business with lucrative orders for equipment.

FARAWAY HAVEN

This view of Sydney Harbour in about 1867 gives an inkling of how slender was the British presence on the edge of the vast Australian continent, and how few and vulnerable were the ships that provided the only lifeline home. The gold rushes of the 1850s had stimulated mass emigration, and the new settlers soon outnumbered the convicts and ex-convicts.

As long as the settlers paid for themselves, the government in Whitehall was quite happy to see them govern themselves, too. New South Wales, Victoria, South Australia and Tasmania (as Van Diemen's Land was renamed) had their own state governments, with parliaments whose lower houses were fully elected. A two-tier empire thus developed, with colonies that were subject to British rule, and white dominions that largely ran their own affairs, often with broader freedoms and more inclusive electorates than in the mother country itself.

MUSICAL MOMENT

The Ritherden family (left) perform a musical interlude in the garden of their colonial home in Madras, India.

INTO THE OUTBACK

The Irish explorer and adventurer Robert Burke (right) set off from Melbourne in August 1860, leading an extravagantly equipped expedition supported by a train of camels. He won the race to become the first to cross Australia from south to north, but did not live to tell the tale.

On the northward journey, Burke decided to leave most of the expedition's stores with an assistant, William Brahe, at Cooper's Creek. He went on with a much smaller group, and in February 1861 they reached the tidal waters of the Flinders River on the Gulf of Carpentaria.

The months went by until Brahe gave the explorers up for lost. He abandoned his post on 21 April, 1861 – just hours before Burke and two exhausted companions staggered back to Cooper's Creek. Burke died there of starvation at the end of June. John King, his only surviving companion, was lucky enough to be kept alive by local Aborigines and was rescued by a relief expedition on September 21.

COURTING CONTROVERSY
Richard Burton (left) and John Speke (below, right) were men of greatly different temperament. Burton was intellectual, artistic and sensuous, a master linguist, poet and the brilliant translator of *The Arabian Nights*. He made a pilgrimage to Mecca, on which he would have been done to death in an instant had his disguise failed him. Speke was a soldier, from an old West Country family, a writer of plodding prose who had served as an Indian Army officer in the Punjab. His great passion was big game hunting. The two shared little other than a love of exploration and adventure.

In 1857 the Royal Geographical Society sent them out to search for the equatorial lakes of central Africa. Together, they discovered Lake Tanganyika (today, Lake Tanzania). Speke, travelling on alone, discovered Lake Victoria and was convinced that the headwaters of the Nile flowed from there. Burton was equally certain that 'his' lake, Tanganyika, was the source. Speke returned with James Grant in 1860 and, on 28 July, 1862, reached the point where the Nile flows from Lake Victoria. He was hailed a hero on his return to London. But Burton questioned the Nile discovery.

The two men were utterly estranged. The day before they were to air their differences, in September 1864, Speke shot himself while partridge shooting on his uncle's estate. Suicide, said those who thought Burton was right. In fact, as later discoveries and events would show, Speke had indeed discovered the source of the Nile, and his death was almost certainly accidental.

THE REDOUBTABLE FLORENCE BAKER

The explorer Samuel White Baker bought his wife Florence (right) in a slave market in the Turkish town of Widden, in what is now Bulgaria, in 1859. She had been born in Hungary, where she was kidnapped as a little girl eleven years before. He took her straight off on his exploration for the sources of the Nile. She proved an excellent travelling companion – 'she had admirable *sang froid*', Baker said, 'she was not a screamer' – and quelled a mutiny among their porters.

Speke and Grant, who had got to the Nile source before the Bakers, were so shocked to meet Florence that they made no mention of her when they returned home. The Bakers went on to look for another great lake that was said to be linked to Lake Victoria. After a gruelling journey, with Florence half-dead of fever and sunstroke, they discovered what they were looking for, in 1864, and named it Lake Albert (today's Lake Albert Nyanza).

When Florence arrived in England in 1865, she found London society as hostile as the African bush. Baker had four children from his first marriage, the eldest only a few years younger than Florence herself. Queen Victoria refused to receive her at court. But Florence won them over. She later accompanied her husband on a dangerous anti-slaving mission in the Nile Basin, marching with 'two bottles of brandy, two drinking cups, and two umbrellas and my pistol in my belt …'.

EMERGING
VALUES

Britain had yet to think of itself as 'Victorian'. But concepts that continue deeply to mark us, and often the wider world, were already emerging in the 1860s. They influence every aspect of everyday life – football as an organised sport, the stiff upper lip, antiseptic surgery – but perhaps the most fundamental is parliamentary democracy.

MIDDLE CLASS MANNERS A woman engaged in needlework in a parlour well-supplied with light and with books, in about 1865.

statesmen' because they made few demands on their MPs' time. He was patronising, too, approving of giving the vote only to those working men whose conduct was 'good enough to entitle them to a share in the privileges of parliamentary representation'. Gladstone proposed to extend the franchise to those who rented property worth £14 a year in the counties and £7 in the towns. He chose the £7 cut-off point because it was 'unattainable by the peasantry and the mere manual labourer'. This fine-tuning, he hoped, would make sure that middle and upper class voters would outnumber the working class by a reassuring six to four.

Even this was too far for some Liberals. The leader of the objecting 'Adullamites' – a Biblical reference to the Adullam cave where 'everyone discontented gathered' – was Robert Lowe. He had spent some time in Australia, and disliked its more open and egalitarian society. He was opposed to anything that smacked of democracy. The reform bill, he said, would empower 'venality … drunkenness … impulsive, unreflecting and violent people …'.

Perhaps because Gladstone was exhausted, working a 14-hour day and snatching naps in the House, the Adullamites were able to combine with the Conservatives to defeat the Bill in June 1866. Russell duly resigned. He was replaced by a Conservative minority government, with Lord Derby as Prime Minister – for the third time – and Disraeli taking over Gladstone's dual tasks. A crowd that gathered in London to protest at Russell's resignation gave warning of the ugly mood that July. Police barred the protesters from Hyde Park, but iron railings were torn down and flower beds trampled in response to the blocking of reform. The scene did not degenerate into a riot, but it was violent enough to persuade Derby and Disraeli that the franchise must be extended.

Disraeli sees it through

Disraeli introduced a new Reform Bill. It was an extraordinary piece of work. Almost a million new voters were enfranchised by it, many more than Gladstone had proposed. Yet Disraeli managed to steer it through the Commons with a majority of 70 against him. Perhaps even more remarkable, he steered it through his own party, for the Conservatives were traditionally much less reform-minded than the Liberals. Tory diehards in the cabinet agreed with Thomas Carlyle, the great historian and sage of the day, that democracy was

PROSPEROUS CITY
The population of Scotland had almost doubled to 3 million from the start of the century to the 1861 census. This scene of Canongate in Edinburgh shows the house of the Calvinist reformer John Knox. Edinburgh was a prosperous city of sober and respectable professionals, in contrast to the burgeoning industrial city of Glasgow, with its shipyards and slums swelling with Irish Catholic immigrants.

mere 'swarmery' and that the bill would cut civilisation loose to 'shoot Niagara'. Even Derby thought it 'a great experiment … a leap in the dark'. Several resigned, which helped Disraeli to camouflage the bill's real intention.

Gladstone's narrower bill, he realised, would have reinforced Liberal strength to the point where the Conservatives faced extinction. Disraeli again and again accepted radical amendments and blocked more modest proposals from Gladstone. He felt that the Conservatives had little to lose. They had not won a parliamentary majority since the Peelite split more than 20 years before: they had lost five general elections on the trot. Disraeli recognised that their best hope of survival was to create an alliance of their traditional supporters in the counties with new working class and middle class Tories in the towns and cities. In his hopes of winning the new working class votes, Disraeli was the first 'One Nation' Tory. In his novel *Sybil*, a stranger tells the hero Egremont that British society was fractured into 'Two Nations, between whom there is no intercourse and no sympathy … formed by a different breeding, fed by different food, ordered by different manners'. To this, Egremont replies, hesitating, 'You speak of … of the rich and poor'. It was this split that radical Tories have ever since tried to bridge.

Disraeli achieved it with subtle brilliance, by reducing Gladstone's property threshold so that more people qualified to vote. His bill more than doubled the number of voters in the borough seats, where instead of one in five, 45 per cent of adult men had the vote. In contrast, in the counties the number crept up by well under half, from 17 per cent to just 24 per cent. The changes seemed radical and opposed to gerrymandering, yet in practice they were calculated to assure the Tories a future. The boroughs were Liberal fortresses, so it made little difference to increase the electorate in them. Disraeli could afford to be less generous in the county seats, where most of the smaller percentage who gained the vote could safely be assumed to vote Tory. The Act was passed in 1867.

WOMEN'S CHAMPION

The philosopher, politician and social reformer John Stuart Mill, with his stepdaughter Helen Taylor. Mill's father – the Scottish philosopher and historian, James Mill – started him on Greek at the age of three, and Latin and mathematics at eight. He was kept apart from other boys, and his only recreation was a walk with his father, who used it for oral tests.

He recovered from a nervous crisis as a young man, probably brought on by his strange upbringing, and flung himself into philosophy and social reform. His essay *On Liberty* defined and defended, with brevity and elegance, individual freedoms against political encroachment. He became an MP in 1865, and fought to improve the status of women, causing much controversy with the publication in 1869 of his work *The Subjection of Women*.

> British society was fractured into 'Two Nations … formed by a different breeding, fed by different food, ordered by different manners … the rich and poor.'
>
> Disraeli, in his novel *Sybil*

The effect on the ground

One in three adult men now had the vote in England nd Wales – Scotland passed its own Act the following year – but the new franchise was hardly ideal. In Ireland, only one in six could vote. London was hugely under-represented, with only a score of MPs, four of them returned by the City elite. And women, who were in a slight majority in the country, were not represented at all.

John Stuart Mill, the social reformer and philosopher, introduced a bill to give the vote to women. It was defeated by 196 votes to 73, a surprisingly small majority against so radical a measure, at a time when, though there were a handful of pioneer feminists, no suffragette movement existed. Nonetheless, the 1867 Act confirmed the country as a parliamentary democracy. Reform, however grudging, flowed from MPs, not from riots and barricades.

Derby retired with ill-health – he had chronic gout – in February 1868, and Disraeli succeeded him as Prime Minister. On kissing Queen Victoria's hand when he took office, he was famously reported to have said: 'I have climbed to the top of the greasy pole.' He did not stay there long.

A thoroughly modern election

A general election was called in December 1868, the first parliamentary election in Britain that was recognisably modern. Fewer seats were uncontested than previously – down to 140 from 240 in the election of 1859. Two great parties with two distinct leaders, Disraeli and Gladstone, battled it out nationwide. Then, as now, the Celtic countries were a disaster for the Tories – Scotland returned 52 Liberals and just eight Tories, while the Wales count was 22 and eight. And then, as now, the English counties were Tory strongholds. Despite Disraeli's franchise reforms, the Liberals won again, with 382 seats to the Conservatives' 276. Gladstone became Prime Minister for the first time.

But there were indicators of the future. The Conservatives increased their strength in the counties, as Disraeli foresaw, and there were signs that the Tory working man was not an illusion. The Tories did better than expected in Lancashire, particularly in Bolton and Salford – and in Manchester, where the first Conservative was elected since the city had been enfranchised in 1832.

A NEW SERVICE
Fire was an ever-present hazard. The Palace of Westminster itself had burned down in 1834, and there were a series of hugely expensive warehouse fires along the banks of the River Thames in 1861. Fire-fighters and fire stations were provided by insurance companies and run by private enterprise. In 1865 Parliament bowed to pressure from the insurers to provide fire cover at public expense, and the Metropolitan Fire Brigade Act created the public fire brigade in the capital.

NEW AND OLD TRADES

The first Trades Union Congress met in 1868, a portent for the future. It was also a reminder that many working men – and all working women – were still excluded from the vote, and were organising themselves to pursue their interests in other ways. The year before, a statistician worked out that just over 10 per cent of the population were 'higher skilled labour' earning £60 to £73 a year. 'Lower skilled labourers', on £46 to £52 a year, made up about 40 per cent. Farm labourers and the unskilled, who accounted for about 30 per cent, earned from £20 to £41.

Engineers building the Albert Embankment in London in 1865 were paid 7 shillings 6d a day. Bricklayers, masons, carpenters and smiths made 6 shillings 6d a day. Excavators, who had to provide their own 'long water boots', earned 4 shillings 6d and common labourers 3 shillings a day. This was for a 10-hour

DIGGING FOR A LIVING
Navvies had moved on from building the canals that gave them their name – a shortened form of 'navigators' – to the railways, and then to sewers and drainage schemes. In 1865 Ford Maddox Brown made a famous painting of them entitled 'Work', which showed them laying the new London sewers in a road in Hampstead. The men above were taking their dinner break from work on an outlet culvert in Yorkshire, not far from Barnard Castle.

FROM REEDS TO ROOFS
Men harvesting reeds on the Norfolk Broads. The reeds were transported by boat on the extensive waterways and used for thatching. Many country cottages had thatched roofs, for reed beds were found in many places, though the craft was at its most resplendent in East Anglia. Much artistry went into creating traditional shapes and patterns that varied greatly between individual thatchers as well as districts.

working day, six days a week, rather than the 11½ hour working day usual among builders before strikes in the early 1860s had won them improved conditions. There was little wage inflation. The 1871 contracts for the men building the Chelsea Embankment were unchanged over the decade, apart from an extra sixpence a day for labourers and a shilling for hard-to-get bricklayers. White collar workers were much better off. An experienced, on-site engineer made about £110 a year, no more than a wet-behind-the-ears civil engineering clerk.

Conditions were slowly improving in industry. In the 1850s, textile workers put in more than 10 hours a day, six days a week, plus 7½ hours on Sundays. By the late 1860s, many did not work on Sundays at all and some had Saturday afternoons free as well. There were still bad spots. London dressmakers employed some 15,000 young girls, brought up from the country. They worked for 10 hours at a stretch in the foul air of the workrooms, and ate and slept on the premises.

Living on the land

Farm labourers – variously known as 'clodhoppers ... chopsticks ... haw bucks ... Johnny Raws' – often had to survive harsh conditions. A farm labourer's son from Saffron Walden in Essex recalled a particularly bitter winter in 1861. 'There was a wonderful large family of us – eleven was born, but we died down to six,' he said. 'One very cold day, we had nothing at all in the house … I took a bag and presently I lit on a farmer, and said to him, "I've come out to ask for a few turnips, sir, if you'll please to give 'em me." "You can go down the field," he says, "and pull some, if you can get 'em up." … The ground was so hard, I was forced to cut 'em out with a bill-hook. When I brought them home we had to thaw them before the fire before we could pare them for boiling.'

Farming was generally stable in the 1860s, though. The wheat price was maintained, but the growing demand for meat, butter and cheese made livestock an attractive proposition. Where the land allowed, farmers shifted from arable to pasture, from 'corn to horn'.

A changing economy

At the start of the century a third of all income stemmed from agriculture, fishing and forestry. By 1861 this was down to 18 per cent, with a further drop to 14 per cent by the end of the decade. Manufacturing, mining and construction, in contrast, had grown from 23 per cent to 36 per cent and hit almost 40 per cent by the end of the decade. Trade and transport climbed more slowly to around

PRIZE BULL
James Anderson with his bull, The Rose of the Suir, which had just won First Prize at the Waterford Show of 1863. The Andersons of Grace Dieu Lodge, the family estate in Co. Waterford, were of old Anglo-Irish stock. James's father had been a rector: the vicarage and rectory were the nurseries of men as varied as Nelson and Lewis Carroll, a resource denied to Catholic countries, with their celibate priests. The British practised primogeniture, too, so that estates were inherited outright by eldest sons. James's brothers had to venture out into the world to earn their living, one as an officer in the Light Dragoons, and another as a Royal Navy commander.

ENGINEERING IN ACTION
Industry peppered the Southeast as well as the Midlands and North. These men are metalworkers at Messrs Rennie's works in Deptford. The Rennie brothers, George and John, were sons of the great bridge-builder John Rennie. They were involved in shipbuilding, railways and bridges, machinery for flour mills, cast iron screws and piles for lighthouses, locomotives and marine engines. They built the *Dwarf*, the navy's first vessel with a screw propeller. Demand for engineering products was high throughout the 1860s. New railways, harbours, docks and bridges were needed abroad as well as at home.

The country was industrially still almost self-sufficient ...

22 per cent. Income from investments abroad, virtually nil throughout the period of the Napoleonic wars, was climbing towards 5 per cent.

The country was industrially still almost self-sufficient. Food and raw materials like cotton accounted for 95 per cent of imports, with manufactured goods at only 5 per cent: the Germans and Americans had yet to hit their industrial stride. Almost half total exports were cotton and woollens. Europe was the most important export market, followed by the USA, Canada and the West Indies. Australia was beginning to figure, though.

Income tax was levied only on incomes above £100 a year. During the 1860s, the rate varied between about 2 per cent and 4 per cent – the maximum was 10 pence in the pound, in 1861 – on incomes above the threshold. London and the southern boroughs had the highest concentrations of men with such incomes. New Windsor was spectacularly rich – men with over £100 a year made up more than 40 per cent of its adult males. Buckingham, Brighton, Gloucester, Guildford and the university towns were also well-heeled. The old commercial towns like Bristol, too, and other places with well-established middle class families like York, were much better off than the new factory towns in the north. Only 10 per cent of men in Leeds enjoyed a £100-plus income. York had double that.

RAW MATERIALS
Skilled workers, splitting slates. Victorian house-building and a vigorous programme of church building helped to guarantee work for craftsmen like these. Stonemasons were also much in demand, often to provide decorative carving for monuments, memorials and gravestones. Cemeteries were so grandly adorned that some became tourist attractions.

THE WOMAN'S LOT

Women were a huge and essential part of the nation's workforce. They outnumbered men in the vital textile industry – the source of half the country's exports – by about 400,000 to 286,000. They were not the shrinking violets of legend. Many, married and single alike, were wage earners: probably most worked, for although the census was accurate enough on the vast numbers of domestic servants and women factory workers, it largely ignored the many thousands who toiled at home. They were the seamstresses and knitters, the straw-plaiters of Bucks and Beds, embroiderers and glove-makers, the London umbrella-makers and dressmakers, the stocking and shoemakers of the Midlands and North, the milliners, the hard-drinking washerwomen, and the fish wives on the coast who mended nets and gutted fish.

> **Women outnumbered men in the vital textile industry – the source of half the country's exports – by about 400,000 to 286,000.**

The maid-of-all-work

Even without home-workers, the 1861 census reported that women made up almost a third of the total workforce, with almost a million working as domestic servants, another 145,000 as washerwomen and 55,000 as charwomen. Most common of all was the general servant, or 'maid-of-all-work', whom Mrs Beeton thought 'the only one of her class deserving of commiseration …'. And small wonder. Mrs Beeton put her through her paces.

She had to 'rise with the lark … open the shutters … brush up the kitchen range, light the fire, clear away the ashes, clean the hearth, polish with a leather the bright parts of the range'. She had then to go to the dining room, to 'shake and fold the tablecloth, sweep the room, clean the grate, dust the furniture' before moving on to the hall, there to 'shake the mats, clean the doorstep and any brass knockers or handles and clean the boots'. She had then to 'cook the bacon, kidneys, fish, etc …'. Whilst the family breakfasted, she darted upstairs to open the bedroom windows and strip off the bedclothes, which would be left to air while she cleared away the family's breakfast things.

And that was merely the start of the day – it finished late in the evening, when she locked and bolted the doors and left wood to dry by the fire – although Mrs Beeton allowed that she might have off 'a short time in the afternoon'.

The governess

Governesses numbered in the tens of thousands. They were in a most sensitive position, employed by parents to teach and train children in the household. A governess, wrote the early feminist Elizabeth Sewell in 1865, was neither a relative, guest, servant or mistress, but 'something made up of all. No one knew exactly how to treat her.' If her father had 'passed through the gazette' – the phrase for

A HARD WORKING LIFE
These young women were employed in a South Wales ironworks in around 1865. Many women performed hard manual work and outnumbered the men in textile factories. In the mines, they sorted coal as 'pit brow lasses'. They toiled as seamstresses and washerwomen, walnut crackers, fish gutters and vegetable pickers. The thousands who worked in match factories suffered 'phossy jaw' from the phosphorus.

continued on page 59

WOMEN IN DOMESTIC SERVICE

The personal lady's maid (left) was part of the Victorian army of maids – kitchen maids, scullery maids, housemaids, nursemaids, parlour maids, maids-of-all-work. The young women below were employed as kitchen staff in a large house near Keswick in the Lake District. Nothing is known of the cheerful-looking maid on the right, other than the date that her picture was taken – 1867.

In the large Victorian household, the butler was the top earner with wages of £40 to £100 a year. Cooks came next,

at £18 to £50. Footmen, chosen as much for their looks as their ability to open a door, made the same as a nursery governess, around £20 to £40. A parlour maid earned between £12 and £30. Board and lodging came free.

About three quarters of a million women were in domestic service. At best, in a happy house, it was a secure and stable interlude between childhood and marriage. At worst, though, the maid-of-all-work was expected to do just that, to toil and drudge from dawn until evening, for a pittance.

MARRIAGE – A SERIOUS MATTER

Social etiquette was of utmost importance to Victorians. Many were the first generation in their family to have social horizons beyond the local town, to be able to entertain, to have servants – or to marry in style. Specialist books and magazines were produced to help them. *The Ladies' and Gentlemen's Model Letter Writer* gave examples of how to accept, refuse or postpone a decision on a proposal of marriage: 'I shall esteem myself happy in having secured the affection of so good a man … as a Friend I shall ever like and esteem you, but I cannot feel for you the love which alone can make married life happy … I am sure I may safely appeal to your generosity for time to give the matter consideration …'.

Most marriages took place in church or chapel. Seven out of ten in England and Wales were held in Anglican churches, two in ten in Nonconformist and other chapels; just 4.3 per cent were in Catholic churches. Fewer than two in a hundred were in registry offices. Generally, the richer and better educated the bride and groom, the older they were to marry, but on average even labourers waited until they were 24 and had enough money to set up a home. Divorce was rare, illegitimacy was less than 5 per cent. Marriages might not be formally 'arranged', but they were often convenient and practical alliances between families.

being declared bankrupt – she might be better bred than the family she served. Like the modern au pair, the head of the family might fancy her. 'Is she handsome or attractive?' wives would ask before hiring. 'If so, it is conclusive against her.'

Unequal rewards and new opportunities

Women in industry earned on average a little less than half what the men got. They usually did the unskilled work in factories – though where they were skilled, like women weavers, they wore hats and gloves to work to show their superiority over the unskilled spinners. They wrapped and packed in the chocolate factories of Bristol and Birmingham. 'Pit brow lasses' got the coal ready for transport from the mines. The 'bait girls' of Scarborough were lowered down the cliffs to gather mussels and winkles.

New fields of employment were opening up. Trained and qualified nurses began to replace self-taught midwives. Woman were an official part of the Army Nursing Service from 1861. The growth of shops and stores created a mass demand for women shop assistants. Derry and Toms opened in Kensington High Street in 1862. William Whiteley, 'the universal provider', set up in Westbourne Grove a year later. By the end of the decade, he was employing 2000. Hard on his heels, John Lewis opened in Oxford Street and Bentall's in Kingston upon Thames. A cricketing family, the Lillywhites, opened a store in London that was soon a temple of sporting goods. In the north, the Co-operative Wholesale Society was founded in 1863, with 3000 members. Soon, half a million had joined 'the Co-op'.

'Parents who intend their daughters to become saleswomen should take care they are thoroughly proficient in arithmetic', Emily Faithfull advised in her 1864 careers book, *Choice of a Business for Girls*. The life was healthier than a dressmaker's, but the girl needed 'entire self-command' to put up with 'unreasonable and rude' customers. Salaries were from £20 to £50 a year, with board and lodging. 'A tall figure is considered an advantage', Emily Faithfull added, 'and the power of standing for many hours is a requisite.'

The burgeoning paperwork and record-keeping in government departments and private companies needed large numbers of clerical staff. The Post Office, for example, employed a growing army of administrative staff. Decorum was preserved in large offices by having separate entrances and staggered lunch hours for male and female clerks.

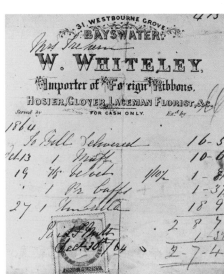

PROOF OF PURCHASE
A receipt from Whiteley's, one of the new breed of department store opening up in London and around the country, dated 1864. The new stores provided a new source of employment for young women as shop assistants. A well-mannered girl with a head for figures and good deportment might earn as much as £50 a year, a substantial sum compared to the £10 a year that a maid-of-all-work might expect.

Teaching absorbed bright, self-confident girls. There were 80,000 women teachers in the 1860s. That had more than doubled by the end of the century. The Cambridge University local examinations were opened to girls in 1863. Scores of girls' grammar schools and Church schools were founded, with a handful of elite boarding schools, Wycombe Abbey, Cheltenham Ladies' College, Roedean. Their purpose, though, was not yet to send girls on to the still closed professions and university – the first girls' college at Cambridge, Girton, was not opened until 1873 – but to produce 'intellectual companions for their brothers, help and counsellors for their husbands, and wise guides for their children'.

For all their growing influence at work, women were discriminated against. If they were married, they had no legal discretion to spend what they earned in wages as they saw fit. In general, under common law all a wife's earnings and possessions belonged to her husband. Only wealthy women enjoyed some protection. Fathers wary of fortune hunters often drew up marriage settlements that allowed their daughters to continue to control their estates after they married, placing their property and private income outside the husband's grasp.

Divorce was difficult, expensive and tipped in the husband's favour. A man could sue purely on grounds of adultery, but a wife had to prove her husband guilty of bestiality, bigamy, incest, rape or cruelty as well. The Church frowned on divorce and it was extremely rare. There were some 190,000 marriages a year in the mid-Victorian era. Only 239 on average ended in divorce.

The oldest profession

A major employer of women that did not appear in the census figures was prostitution. Estimates of numbers varied enormously – from 20,000 to 150,000 in London alone. The great Russian novelist Fyodor Dostoyevsky knew the dark side of Russian cities, but he was amazed by London. Around the Haymarket, he wrote in 1863, 'prostitutes swarm by night in their thousands … glistening, expensive clothes and semi-rags and sharp differences in age … curses, quarrels, solicitations and the quiet whispered invitation …'.

The high incidence of venereal disease among soldiers and sailors led to the first Contagious Diseases Act in 1864. Prostitutes in garrison towns and seaports who refused to be examined by a doctor could be imprisoned for six months. It was fiercely opposed by radicals, like the philosopher and writer John Stuart Mill, and Josephine Butler, the formidable social reformer, and wife of the canon of Winchester.

The ultimate cause of prostitution, Josephine Butler wrote, was precisely this Victorian 'double standard', the 'doctrine that impurity in man is a slight and excusable offence, while in a woman it is a deadly and unpardonable sin'. She had formidable energy. She nursed prostitutes in her Liverpool house, and looked after sick sailors, too, proud that 'no loathsome attribute of the disease ever kept me and other ladies away from this labour of love'.

Butler went on a famous 'warfare among the foreigners' tour of Europe. In Paris, she dubbed the French equivalent to the

MEANS TO AN END
A trade card advertising sewing needles shows a fashionably dressed lady pulling prosperous gentlemen onto her thread. For most women, obtaining a husband was the only route to security. But such security came at a price. On marriage all that a woman possessed became the property of her husband. Fashion had a high price, too, for the workers who produced it. The lungs of the fur pullers who prepared rabbit skins filled with fine rabbit down that left them breathless. The chemicals in the dyes used in artificial flowers slowly poisoned the women who made them. Tuberculosis was rampant in the dank, airless and crowded rooms where seamstresses worked.

1864 Act, the 'Morals' Service', as the 'Service of Debauchery'. She helped form the British, Continental and General Federation for the Abolition of Government Regulation of Prostitution. Her genius was to make prostitution a matter of public decency and moral standards, not of simple repression, and to make people conscious of 'the unequal standard of morality for the sexes'.

Many of the 'fallen women' in London were in fact unfortunate victimised children. A member of the Society for the Rescue of Young Women, who appealed to readers of *The Times* for funds in 1864, said that only 33 of 472 girls in the society's care had started out as prostitutes after the age of 21. The greatest number were 14 and 15 year olds, but 57 were pre-teenagers, two of them eight-year olds. Very few were born Londoners. Most were country girls who had lost one or both parents. The number of children driven to the streets of London, the society said, 'is almost beyond belief'.

This early feminism, and the demand for fair treatment for all women, had another great champion in J S Mill. He had already urged that women be given the vote, and he wrote on *The Subjection of Women* in 1869. 'A woman born to the present lot of women, and content with it, how should she appreciate the value of self-dependence?' he asked. 'Her familiar notions of good are of blessings descending from a superior.'

ANGLO-FRENCH COURTESAN
The birth certificate of Cora Pearl gave 1842 as her year of birth and Plymouth as the place. It was most likely forged, and that she was born in London seven years earlier. Her real name was Emma Crouch and her father, a cellist and composer, abandoned the family. Emma set out to live off her wits. She was not a great beauty, but she was lively, witty, intelligent and good company. She was known as La Lune Rousse, for her red hair and moon-shaped face. She became the mistress of a London restaurateur, who took her to Paris, which she adored. Its rich men adored her. She had affairs with the Duke of Rivoli, the painter Gustav Doré and Prince Napoleon, who bought her a house so opulent it was compared to a royal palace. She left Paris during the Franco-Prussian war, but returned after the Grosvenor Hotel refused her admission. Eventually, her fortunes waned and she died in poverty.

HEALTH AND HOLIDAYS

There were auguries in the physical as well as constitutional health of the nation. Victoria might be the grandest monarch on Earth, but early in the decade she had lost her husband to typhoid – a disease most commonly caused by drinking infected water – and her eldest son came within a whisker of sharing the same fate. By the decade's end, progress had been made in understanding how infections were contracted. In London Sir Joseph Bazalgette was building state-of-the-art sewers to carry away waste, freeing the city from some deadly waterborne diseases that over the centuries had carried off scores of thousands.

A DAY AT THE BEACH A family takes advantage of lobster pots round a boat for seats on the beach at Swanage, Dorset.

TACKLING DISEASE

Proper sewers underpin the public health, and they are a mid-Victorian legacy of hugely under-rated importance. That is partly, of course, because they are out of sight, although London's noble Embankments along the Thames were built as part of Joseph Bazalgette's grandiose scheme. Mainly, though, it is because sewers are out of mind: we no longer think of them as the lifesavers they are precisely because men like Bazalgette have allowed us to lose our terror of diseases such as typhoid and cholera.

Bazalgette's work is literally a legacy. London still relies on his sewers, despite its huge growth in population. Not only did he build them well, he deliberately built them oversize. To calculate the diameter of pipe needed, he allowed for the maximum amount of waste per Londoner, and then he doubled it, commenting: 'We're only going to do this once and we must allow for the unforeseen.'

Water and disease

Cholera had come from India, where the first pandemic had broken out in 1817. The deadly disease first arrived in Britain in 1831, brought by seamen, soldiers or merchants returning from Bengal. The fever led swiftly to dehydration and death. There were three more major cholera outbreaks in Britain, in 1849, 1853 and 1866. The last two killed 16,000 in London alone.

It was soon noted that outbreaks of the disease often started near docks, but it was believed at first that it was the vile air of cities – the 'miasma' – that carried cholera and other infections. In fact, as the epidemiologist Dr John Snow realised, it was spread by contaminated water. Snow, like Bazalgette, is another Victorian whose genius is often forgotten today. He was also a pioneer of anaesthetics, and administered chloroform to Queen Victoria during the birth of Prince Leopold, then a radical procedure. Snow traced one cholera outbreak in London to a water pump in Soho that was contaminated with raw sewage. He also realised the dangers posed by the Thames, which even though thick with sewage was drawn on by many for domestic water.

The final straw

'King Cholera' induced such fear that journals like *The Lancet* were criticised even for reporting on it. The government, always short of spare funds, was reluctant to act, but the hot summer of 1858 finally convinced them that something must be done. The river was so filthy that when the first steam packets began stirring the water with their propellers soon after dawn, the smell was 'enough to strike down strong men'. At night, when there was little traffic, the 'heavy matter sinks, but the renewed agitation in the morning causes the escape of pungent gases'. Even the dipping of oars 'produces a sickening sensation'. The 'Great Stink' during the 1858 heat wave was so foul that Parliament and other riverside buildings were rendered uninhabitable. The government at last passed an enabling act to carry out a spectacular scheme put forward by Joseph Bazalgette.

To tackle the stench and miasma, Bazalgette proposed dealing directly with the sewage outflows that caused it – and thus with waterborne disease, too. The great

AN ENGINEER FOR TOMORROW
Joseph Bazalgette was the son of a Royal Navy captain. He was a brilliant engineer who learnt the practicalities of land reclamation and drainage as a railway builder. He was appointed chief engineer to the Metropolitan Board of Works (MBW) in London in 1855. He sounds worthy but dull. He was not. The sewers and drains that he built saved life on an epic scale. He had foresight: he deliberately overbuilt to provide capacity for population growth. He had civic pride and taste: he created the magnificent Embankments that transformed the Thames in the heart of the capital from an ill-defined stretch of noxious, flood-prone water into a noble promenade. Even the pumping stations of his sewerage system were designed with as much care as campaniles.

When the MBW was empowered to buy the Thames bridges from private companies, and free them from tolls, Bazalgette designed and built the masonry arch bridge at Putney, the Hammersmith suspension bridge and the iron arch Battersea Bridge, all of which still stand. He planned great thoroughfares – Charing Cross Road, Shaftesbury Avenue, Queen Victoria Street – to relieve congestion.
He was a man equal to the times.

Victorian engineers did not do things by halves, and Bazalgette was no exception. He set about constructing in brick underground main sewers to carry the main outflows, plus hundreds of miles of under-street sewers that fed into these, carrying the rainwater and sewage that had previously flowed through London's thoroughfares.

As part of the scheme, Bazalgette also built the great Embankments of central London – Chelsea, Albert, Victoria – that reclaimed the meandering, tide-wracked banks of the river and transformed them into handsome esplanades, embellished with granite steps and gas lamps finely cast in the shape of dolphins. The architectural elegance continued in the great pumping stations that Bazalgette built as part of the scheme, at Abbey Mills, the Lea Valley, the Erith marshes and the Chelsea Embankment.

continued on page 72

Cholera arrived in Britain in 1831 … and there were three more major outbreaks – in 1849, 1853 and 1866. The last two killed 16,000 in London alone.

VOICE OF WISDOM

Edwin Chadwick (right) campaigned against squalor and disease all his life. He attributed the high disease and mortality rate of the poor to the gross inadequacies or non-existence of drainage, water supplies and sanitary facilities in the slums. He pressured the government to set up a national health authority, the General Board of Health. Benjamin Richardson was another pioneer of the sanitary movement. He was a physician who investigated cholera, invented the first double-valve mouthpiece for administering chloroform to patients undergoing surgery, and discovered 14 new anaesthetics. He also wrote plays, biographies, poems and a three-volume romantic novel. The indefatigable polymath was a distinct Victorian character.

BUILDING LONDON'S SEWERS

The scale of Joseph Bazalgette's sewage and drainage scheme for London was epic: some 1300 miles of below-street sewers, which drained into 82 miles of main west-east intercepting sewers. The waste drained eastwards along these by gravity to pumping stations at Abbey Mills, in West Ham on the north side of the river, and at Crossness on the south side. Here, the waste was pumped into the outfall sewers that released it into the Thames at high tide. The new system was a huge success in cleaning up the capital, but the shortcoming of the scheme was that it had simply moved the problem downstream.

TUNNELS TO LAST
These three huge tunnels are part of the northern outfall sewer being built below the Abbey Mills pumping station, which served the city north of the river. Chief engineer Joseph Bazalgette, standing top right, is surveying progress. The northern system was running by 1868, and the whole was finished seven years later. London's waste still travels down these Victorian tunnels, but it is no longer released into the river.

UNEXPECTED PROBLEM

Construction of the middle level sewer under Church Street in Shoreditch, East London (below), was interrupted by a gas explosion in 1862, which caused the timber props over the sewer to collapse (bottom). Bazalgette overcame innumerable challenges to give the world's largest city a sewage and drainage system that worked.

BUILDING MATERIALS

The amount of materials consumed by the project was staggering. These concrete mills (right) below the Abbey Mills pumping station were turning out concrete that went into the northern outfall sewer. Meanwhile, brickworks all over London worked hard to supply the demand.

A different approach

In the prevalence of disease, the Victorians had changed little since their ancestors. They lived little longer – indeed, in the new industrial slums they were actually dying younger. It is the way that they dealt with sickness that distinguishes the Victorians and leaves us in their debt. The foundation of a sharp improvement in public health were laid now – Joseph Lister's antiseptic system, like Bazalgette's sewers, was a product of the decade. Introduced in 1867, it revolutionised modern surgery, but it took time for it to bear fruit. Life expectancy was some 40 years at the start of the century. By 1860 it had limped up to 42, but it was not until the end of Victoria's reign that the 50 milestone was reached.

It was neither sugary sentimentality nor a taste for the macabre that made Victorian novelists and painters deal so much with early death. Rather, it reflected the grim reality. 'I learn from the statistical tables that one child in five dies within the first year of its life; and one in three within the fifth,' Dickens wrote in *The Uncommercial Traveller*. 'That don't look as if we could never improve in these particulars, I think!'

Common killers and dangerous practices

Birth was extremely dangerous, for mother as well as child: Mrs Beeton, of cookery book fame, died after the birth of her fourth child. Infancy was a critical period. Cow's milk was often infected. So was the water in the pap – bread and water dipped in sugar or treacle – that was fed to infants.

Medical officers complained of the habit of dosing fractious babies with narcotics to quieten them. Laudanum, a tincture of opium, was commonly used. It cost a penny an ounce, about the same as a pint of beer, and it was sold quite legally in town and country. It was thought that five out of six working class families in Manchester used it on a regular basis. The records of one druggist in the city showed that each week he was selling half a gallon of the popular Godfrey's Cordial – a potent mix of opium, treacle, water and spices – plus five or six gallons of other 'quieteners'.

Steedman's Powder and Atkinson's Royal Infants Preservative were other high-selling proprietary brands. A respectable druggist in Nottingham, who was also a town councillor, was selling 400 gallons of laudanum a year. Opium in pills and penny sticks sold so widely in East Anglia that it was described as a way of life there. It was drunk throughout the Fens in 'poppy tea', and doctors were shocked at how it wasted the infants, 'shrunk up like little old men … wizened like little monkeys'. But it was starvation rather than overdose that was the common killer. A Privy Council investigation found how children 'kept in a permanent state of continued narcotism will be thereby disinclined for food, and be but imperfectly nourished'. Marasmus, or general emaciation, and death from malnutrition followed.

Infectious diseases were the big killers of those who survived early childhood. Typhus was spread by body lice, and the unwashed poor were most affected. But typhoid, diphtheria, scarlet fever and cholera affected all classes. Tuberculosis, or TB, was a particular scourge. It was the 'family attendant' of the Brontës – two of the three literary sisters, Anne and Emily, had died of the disease. The poet and novelist George MacDonald lost his mother, father, brother and half-sister to TB, and then four of his own children. Small wonder that death appears even in his children's books.

ANTISEPTIC PIONEER
Even though he had been preceded by the likes of William Harvey and Edward Jenner – respectively, the discoverer of the circulation of the blood and the pioneer of vaccination – Joseph Lister (above) was the first medical man to be raised to the peerage in recognition of his achievements. His father was a microscopist, from Essex, which perhaps inspired the son with his interest in micro-organisms.

Lister worked as a surgeon at Edinburgh Royal Infirmary and then Glasgow Infirmary in an age when surgery was often quickly followed by gangrene or other infection. The belief at the time was that these were caused by a 'miasma' or chemicals in the air. But Lister knew from the work of the Frenchman Louis Pasteur that, if microbes were present, an infection could begin even if a wound was not exposed to air. He realised that the infections might be caused by micro-organisms, which in turn might be vulnerable to chemicals.

Carbolic acid was a well-known disinfectant and Lister experimented by spraying it onto surgical instruments, incisions and dressings. When he found that this greatly reduced the incidence of fatal infection, he wrote a series of articles on the use of antiseptics in surgery which were published in *The Lancet* in 1867.

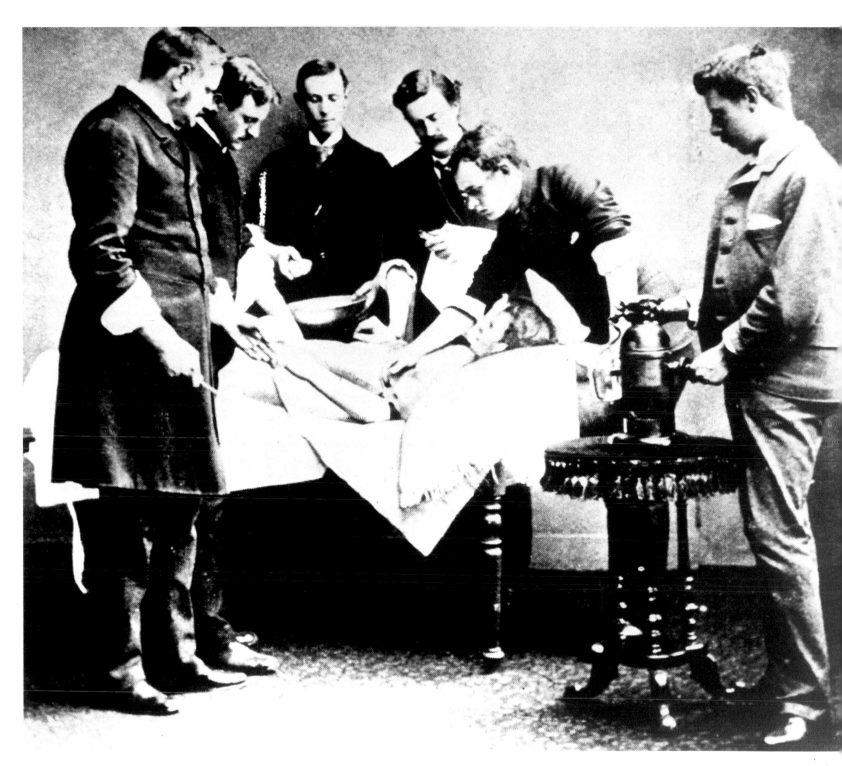

Lister's antiseptic system …
revolutionised modern surgery,
but it took time to bear fruit.

STEP IN THE RIGHT DIRECTION
A carbolic spray being used here to combat
infection during an operation. Lister's
'antiseptic system' required surgeons and
theatre staff to wear clean gloves and to
wash their hands before and after
operations in a 5 per cent carbolic acid
solution. The antiseptic revolution had
begun, but the surgeons were still dressed
in street clothes.

SEASIDE PIERS

The master builder of piers was Eugenius Birch, who, in the multi-talented way of the age, was also a magnificent watercolourist, the builder of Exmouth Docks and the designer of harbours, waterworks and railway bridges on the line from Calcutta to Delhi. Birch built his first pier at Margate in 1853, shown here (right) in a photograph taken in 1860, and his last at Plymouth in 1884, having worked his way around the coast of England erecting 14 in all. Most of them – Blackpool, Brighton, Hastings, Eastbourne, Scarborough – went up in the 1860s using a screw pile technique that he perfected at Margate.

The engineering was ingenious: the piers were attached to the seabed with patented cast-iron screw piles. The first pile for Eastbourne pier (top left) was driven into the seabed in 1866. Because Eastbourne is exposed to the full fury of Channel gales, Birch sat the piles in special cups set into the rock bed, enabling the structure to move in violent weather. The shore end of the 1000-foot long pier was washed away in a storm on New Year's Day 1877, but it was rebuilt at a higher level and the pier remains in use to this day.

Piers reflected the intimate relations of an island people with the sea, enabling day-visiting promenaders to imagine they were walking the deck of an ocean-going ship. They were also venues for mass entertainment, with concert halls, theatres, bandstands, sideshows and landing stages for steamers. As such, they were a relatively cheap but vital accessory for the new seaside resorts. Birch brought Blackpool's North Pier in for £13,500 in 1863. The £30,000 that went on Brighton's West Pier (bottom left) three years later reflected the elegant wrought-iron kiosks and glass screens that protected the resort's well-heeled visitors from Channel winds.

The 1860s was the great decade of building piers, curious structures that jut out into the briny, where promenaders could imagine they were walking the deck of an ocean-going ship.

the mineral waters. Railways had now brought the seaside within reach, and people flocked to brand-new resorts, the brave to swim, others to take donkey rides on the beach, to watch Punch-and-Judy shows and pierrots, to take a steam launch round the bay and to visit the piers, those curious structures where promenaders could imagine they were walking the deck of an ocean-going ship.

Each resort had its own social ethos: Eastbourne and Bournemouth were consciously genteel, while Blackpool promoted the fun of the fair. But everyone enjoyed the sea air – the Victorians loved all things 'bracing' – and the elaborate winter gardens and theatres that resorts invested in to prolong the season.

For this was big business. Ventnor, for example, a small fishing village on the Isle of Wight, was transformed by the opening of the railway in 1866. It turned from rural backwater to flourishing resort, complete with botanical gardens and 'Mediterranean promenade'. Big money went on the hotels. Brighton's huge Grand Hotel was opened in 1864 at a cost of £130,000, a necessary investment to attract a clientele a cut above those who stayed in the boarding houses.

The scale was immense. Bass, the giant brewer in Burton-on-Trent, organised the first of its works outings in 1865. Ten thousand workers and their families were taken on fleets of trains to the resorts, so many that only Blackpool, New Brighton, Scarborough and Great Yarmouth could cope.

FAMILY OUTINGS

Victorian holidays were spent by the water, be it in the Lake District (above) or by the sea. Heavy Victorian clothes and the absence of lifejackets made a boat trip on the lake more of an adventure than it would be now. Not many people could swim.

On Brighton beach in 1866 (right), the bathing machines acted as changing rooms to preserve the modesty of ladies. They could also be pushed right down to the water's edge so that bathers could step directly into the sea without having to walk over the beach. Many of the ladies are holding umbrellas – not to protect them from rain, but to keep out of the sun. A suntan was a mark of the lowest classes, who laboured outdoors, and so was to be avoided. Sunbathing was unheard of: the sea air was the thing, not the sun.

SPORTING PASSIONS

It was characteristic of the Victorian Age to see moral value and social betterment in a humble garden. A similar attitude was reflected in a growing fascination with games. The 1860s is the premier decade for the invention, adaptation and codification of sports. In the public schools, sport was encouraged as a way of teaching boys to be team players, building qualities deemed more important than knowledge of science or industry. *Mens sana in corpore sano*, the motto ran: 'A healthy mind in a healthy body'.

READY, STEADY, ROW A lone oarsman in front of his university boat house in 1868. The sport was introduced at Oxford in the 18th century.

WRITING THE RULES

Cricket was so much more than something simply to be enjoyed. 'It's more than a game. It's an institution.' the hero Tom says to a master as they watch a match in *Tom Brown's Schooldays*. The master describes it as 'noble', for it teaches 'discipline and reliance on one another … It merges the individual in the eleven, he doesn't play that he may win, but that his side may win.' The game had, in short, a moral purpose – and one that, in fostering team spirit, was particularly useful for a far-flung empire. 'Not letting the side down' on a storm-wracked ship or in a lonely and besieged fort was even more important than it was on the cricket field.

Cricket was well established by the 1860s – 'the birthright of British boys old and young', Tom's friend Arthur says – but it was still developing. An English side went to Australia in 1861–2, the first to do so (the very first overseas tour had been to America in 1859). The county championship dates from 1864, the year that Wisden's, the cricketing almanac, was first published. W G Grace, the game's great superstar, began playing for Gloucestershire as a teenager in 1864, following in his brother's footsteps.

> ## Cricket teaches 'discipline and reliance on one another … It merges the individual in the eleven, he doesn't play that he may win, but that his side may win.'
> ### *Tom Brown's Schooldays*

The distinction between amateurs and professionals was already old: the first annual 'gentlemen' against 'players' match had taken place back in 1806, and a professional All-England XI had toured the country. W G Grace is reckoned to be the first modern cricketer. He was arguably the first 'shamateur'. He was a Gentleman Player, using a different dressing room and entrance gate to the humble Players. This official amateur status did not prevent the great man from making a fortune estimated at £120,000 from the game during his long career.

A great divide

The two great winter games were also taking shape. A meeting of eleven football clubs was held in the Freemason's Tavern in Great Queen Street, London, on 26 October, 1863. This was the first meeting of the Football Association.

Fierce argument raged over the rules. In Rugby School rules, players could run with the ball carried in hand and opponents could be 'hacked over' – short for kicked in the shins, tripped or tackled. Enthusiasts of the old 'Cambridge rules' favoured the dribbling game and wanted hacking outlawed. A Rugby rules enthusiast claimed that this would 'do away with all the courage and pluck in the game'. If it was done, he threatened 'I will bring over a lot of Frenchmen who would beat you with a week's practice'.

The two codes split. The ball-carrying hackers withdrew from the FA, eventually to form the Rugby Football Union. The clubs that wanted the dribbling

continued on page 93

PUBLIC SCHOOL FOOTBALL
Players in the 1867 Harrow Soccer Eleven strike a pose in their team strip in front of the school's Gothic windows. Harrow favoured the 'Cambridge rules' version of football, using a round ball.

HOME SCHOOLING
Two boys at a writing desk in 1867. Many children from wealthy families were still taught by tutors and governesses at home. The public schools were expanding rapidly, and tutors were losing out as more and more boys were sent away as boarders. Governesses continued to teach girls the accomplishments that their social status demanded: the three Rs, French or another language, poetry and a grounding in the piano and watercolouring. The governess lived in a sort of limbo, neither servant nor member of the family.

the start of the 19th century, education was the preserve of a few public schools and dame schools, local charitable and voluntary schools, and private governesses and tutors. By 1865, Ragged Schools were giving 27,000 of the poorest children in London a 'plain but sound education'. Penny banks, refuges giving destitute lads and girls shelter with supper and breakfast, and Shoe-Black Brigades were connected to the schools. London had eight brigades, with 350 uniformed boys in each, echoing the cry: 'Have your boots blacked, sir? – only one penny!'

The children were not easy to teach. 'In decency of behaviour, or in discipline of any kind, they are totally unparalleled', a Ragged School teacher complained. 'It were an easier task to get attention from savages.' As soon as he led them into the first verse of the evening hymn, a 'blackguard boy' started off:

Oh, Susannah, don't you cry for me,
I'm off to Alabama, with a banjo on my knee!

All the boys followed his lead – 'aye, girls and all' – and there were even catcalls during the Lord's Prayer. All the copy books were stolen.

Elementary education

For all that, an observer thought that Ragged Schools 'rank deservedly high'. A typical school in London had '300 or 350 of the most ragged and destitute children' packed into a single room. But the teacher, a Mr Fraser, 'never seems to fail. He picks out some of the elder ones to act as monitors, and with the aid of

SCHOOL GROUP
The children at the school in Down Amney in Gloucestershire, in about 1860. Girls had the same chance of a primary education as boys, and women teachers outnumber the men. The vicar of Down Amney, the Reverend Greville Phillimore, was an enlightened and progressive man and is likely to have ensured high standards at the school. Two of his brothers were MPs and another was a Royal Navy commander. He himself had been at Westminster School and Christ Church, Oxford (where another brother had drowned trying to save a companion). Simple country villages were kept in contact with new ideas and learning through well-educated vicars.

female teachers for the girls, he manages to get on very comfortably … Good order prevailed. Some of them can read and write well, particular attention being paid to those essential branches of education.' An impressive collective effort went into the school. Spare food was donated by employees in a nearby company. The children brought spinning tops and balls to play with after school hours, and they were proud of their achievements.

A revised education code in 1862 gave the government control of the basic syllabus in schools. Grants to schools were made dependent on satisfactory child performance and attendance. Tests of proficiency by schools inspectors were carried out, based on what were known – with unashamed poor spelling – as 'the three Rs': reading, writing and arithmetic.

The Elementary Education Act passed at the end of the decade set up School Boards across the country to provide 'public elementary schools' to fill the gaps in the voluntary system. The boards had powers to levy rates, to build new schools and to appoint teachers. They could make attendance compulsory for 5 to 10 year olds, with some exceptions allowed for 10 to 13 years olds, and they could waive fees for parents who could not afford the usual 30 shillings a year per child.

The school boards were the first institutions to be elected by all ratepayers, women included. In another radical move, the 'Cowper-Temple clause' – named for a venerable backbench MP whom Gladstone could not ignore – excluded teaching that was 'distinctive of any particular religious denomination'. In effect, this limited the teaching of religion in Board Schools to Bible-reading and

unknowable – to describe his view that he was open-minded on whether God existed or not. As a member of the London Schools Board he worked to improve the teaching of biology and science. Later he joined forces with the Harrow School master, the Reverend Farrar, to plead for the classics-dominated public schools to take science more seriously. He thought that liberalism, industry and Darwinism, as he called Darwin's evolutionary theories, were vital to national survival. His audiences should cherish science, he told them, or 'see the glory of England vanishing like Arthur in the mist'.

Bishop Samuel Wilberforce fought the Creationists' corner. He was the son of William Wilberforce, leading light in the abolition of slavery. Those who mocked Darwin concentrated on the notion that Man was related to the ape, and it was with heavy sarcasm that Wilberforce asked Huxley whether 'it was through his grandfather or grandmother that he claims his descent from a monkey?' Huxley whispered that 'the Lord has delivered him into my hands', and he rose to reply. 'The question is put to me,' he said, 'would I rather have a miserable ape for a grandfather or a man highly endowed by nature … yet who employs these faculties for the mere purpose of introducing ridicule into a grave scientific discussion. I unhesitatingly affirm my preference for the ape.' There was uproar, a woman fainted. Huxley won the day.

THEATRE AND ENTERTAINMENT

Entertainment, at least, was egalitarian. The Royal Gardens in London claimed to be 'the noblest among all places in England, or the Continent, or in any part of the habitable world'. The programme one July night in 1861 began with Mr d'Alberte, the 'English Rope-Walker and Blondin's Challenger', performing his feat on an illuminated rope high above the crowds. Miss Harriet Coveney sang, followed by an instrumental concert, a ballet-pantomime in six tableaux, a circus troupe of 'educated dogs and monkeys', and a recital by a Swiss lady. Displays of horsemanship were performed in a great circus tent, and Signor Buona Core, the 'Italian salamander or fire king', swallowed swords and ate fire before the finale, a Grand Display of Fireworks. All this could be enjoyed for a shilling a head.

Music halls had the same rich variety of acts. All manner of appearances were made: by champion skaters, shipwrecked sailors, clog-dancers, 'Mexican boneless wonders' or contortionists, conjurers, ventriloquists, bearded ladies and 'equilibrists' who performed amazing balancing acts. Several halls had stages big

A NIGHT AT THE THEATRE
Neither ladies nor gentlemen removed their hats at the theatre, even in an age of big hats and toppers. The theatre was ever more affordable and popular, and about to enter a golden age. The live performance caught here took place in 1863.

STARS OF THE STAGE

Ellen Terry (below), the third of eleven children of theatrical parents, first went on stage when she was eight. By 1863 she was a teenage Titania in *A Midsummer Night's Dream*, displaying remarkable poise, beauty and talent. Shortly before her 17th birthday, in 1864, she married the eminent but far older artist George Watts. It was a disaster, but she survived to launch a dazzling career that saw her work with Henry Irving, George Bernard Shaw, J M Barrie and Herbert Beerbohm Tree. Eventually, she embraced the cinema age and was still making films in 1922.

Henry Irving (right) was the greatest English actor of his age. This picture shows him in 1868 as 'Jingle' from *The Pickwick Papers*. Irving was born in Somerset and worked as a clerk in London before making his first stage appearance in Sunderland. He was in Manchester from 1860 to 1865, and made his London debut at St James's theatre in 1866. He had great stage presence, a genius for subtle characters and emotions, and longevity. Irving and Terry would share a famous partnership at the Lyceum – which he leased as actor-manager – but this was still some years off.

enough for full-scale ballets. The Canterbury, in Westminster Bridge Road in London, had a roof that opened for ventilation on hot summer nights. Performances usually lasted from 8pm to 11.30pm, with admission costing between sixpence and three shillings. The best-heeled hired private boxes.

The 'penny gaff' was at the low end of the market. A simple room was devoted to singing, dancing, comic turns, mimes and 'horrible murder tableaux', depicting the latest and most sensational crimes, forerunners of the elaborate waxworks in Madame Tussaud's Chamber of Horrors. Amid the thick tobacco fumes, a journalist noted in 1861, one penny gaff was home to 'a piano, a seedy gentleman with a violin … and a remarkable easy and assured but debauched looking young man who sings comic songs …'.

Photography – the new medium

Photography boomed. The 51 professional photographers recorded in the 1851 census had mushroomed to 2534 just ten years later. Photography was seen as a great leveller. The rich lost their monopoly of ancestral portraits, previously painted expensively in oils, because the photograph brought the portrait within ordinary reach. *Photographic News* claimed in 1861 that photography had 'swept away many of the illiberal distinctions of rank and wealth'. Jane Carlyle, wife of the historian and sage Thomas Carlyle, thought it an even better invention than chloroform. 'It has given more positive pleasure to poor suffering humanity than anything that has cast up in my time.'

The outstanding photographer of the decade was Julia Margaret Cameron. She was an eager amateur, and used the coalshed at her villa on the Isle of Wight as a darkroom. Her portraits capture poets, scientists, artists' models and parlour maids with equal gusto. Her sitters could be as critical then as they might be now. 'I want to do a large photograph of Tennyson and he objects!', she bemoaned. 'Says I make bags under his eyes…'. In 1872 she photographed Alice Liddell, then a 20 year old of some beauty. It was with this same Alice that ten years earlier another pioneer photographer, Charles Dodgson, had taken a boat trip and picnic 'all in the golden afternoon'. Dodgson was an Oxford mathematics don who, inspired by little Alice and of the stories he had begun telling her at the picnic, wrote of her imagined adventures and meetings with fantastical characters – the March Hare, Tweedledum and Tweedledee, Humpty Dumpty, the Cheshire Cat. *Alice's Adventures in Wonderland* was published in 1865 under the pen-name Lewis Carroll, illustrated by John Tenniel; it was followed by *Through the Looking Glass*. They have since appeared in innumerable editions and languages, in film and on the stage, with a lightness, charm and humour missing from Dodgson's nervous and arid private life.

Cameron practised her art indoors, but itinerant photographers prowled parks and public gardens to take pictures of passers-by. In London they flocked to Clapham Common, a favourite place for pram-pushing nurses to take the children and babies in their care. Photographs here cost as little as a shilling apiece, because there was no expensive studio to maintain, and the price was well within the pocket of families living near the Common. Some photographers would take one of a nurse with child for free, confident that the parents would commission the nurse to buy several more the next time she was perambulating on the Common.

continued on page 121

PHOTOGRAPHY – A NEW ART

By the 1860s photography had brought art to the masses, allowing them to record family faces. *Photographic News* claimed in 1861 that: 'Photographic portraiture is the best feature of the fine arts for the millions that the ingenuity of man has yet devised.' Among the thousands of photographers now plying their trade, a few were genuine artists achieving astonishing results with the still relatively primitive equipment at their disposal.

ARTISTIC TALENTS

The outstanding photographer of the 1860s was Julia Margaret Cameron, who specialised in portraiture. The ethereal lady on the right was her niece, Julia Jackson, photographed in 1866. Cameron's portraits included famous poets, scientists and actors of the day, as well as friends, relatives and ordinary people. She seemed to capture the inner beauty of her sitters, but not all of them agreed – Tennyson accused her of giving him bags under his eyes. The image of four young women in Pre-Raphaelite-like guise (left) is also one of Cameron's.

Francis Frith (below), in a typically bohemiam portrait, was another photographic pioneer. Frith travelled up and down the country taking photographs of towns and villages, eventually amassing an enormous collection. He sold his photographs from his studio in Reigate to 2000 shops nationwide, as an early form of picture postcard.

MURDERERS, THIEVES AND CON ARTISTS

KILLER ON A TRAIN

Franz Muller (left), a German tailor, was convicted in 1864 of the first murder recorded on a train. On the night of 9 July that year, when the 9.50pm train from Fenchurch Street arrived at Hackney station, bloodstains and a beaver hat were found in one of the first class carriages. Thomas Briggs, the chief clerk of a City bank, was found lying severely injured by the track, and his gold watch and chain were missing. He died later in hospital.

A dramatic transatlantic chase then followed. The hat was recognised as belonging to Muller, who sold the gold chain to a jeweller, then on 15 July left for New York aboard the sailing ship *Victoria*. On 20 July a police inspector followed on the steamer *City of Manchester*, but the *Victoria* had such a slow passage that by the time Muller arrived, the inspector had been waiting for him in New York for three weeks. The gold watch was found on him. He was promptly extradited and brought back to London, where he was tried and found guilty at the Old Bailey.

On 14 November, 1864, Muller was hanged in public among such disgraceful scenes of drunkenness that an Act was passed four years later requiring executions to be carried out behind prison walls. Another result of the case was the compulsory fitting of communication cords in train carriages under the Railways Act of 1868, so that passengers could alert the guard in emergencies.

There was crime in plenty, but the overall rate was falling, to 250 indictable offences per 100,000 population – a figure that is 40 times higher today – and this at a time of great individual hardship. Nonetheless, there were some infamous cases in the decade, some of which made history.

POISONER PRITCHARD

The medical qualifications of the 'Regrettable Dr Edward Pritchard' were somewhat dubious, but he became a GP in Glasgow after serving as an assistant surgeon in the navy. He is seen here (left) in happier times in a photograph of about 1860, with his wife, mother-in-law and five children. In 1863 a maid in Pritchard's house was found dead in her room following a fire. Investigation showed that she had made no attempt to flee and Dr Pritchard was suspected of drugging her, but he won his claim to benefit from a life insurance company.

The following year, his wife became ill with vomiting and dizziness. Her mother came to nurse her, but she too fell ill, and both women died within a month of one another in early 1865. Dr Pritchard filled out the death certificates himself, stating that his wife had died of gastric fever and his mother-in-law of apoplexy. Tongues wagged. The bodies were exhumed and evidence of antimony poisoning was found. Dr Pritchard was tried and convicted of the double murder. He was the last person to be hanged in public in Glasgow: his execution, in July 1865, was watched by a crowd estimated at 100,000.

LINE UP OF THIEVES

An early police photograph (below), taken in Glasgow in 1865, shows from left James Lindsay, a 'Dirty Thief'; pickpockets James Cummings and Peter Hasson; and John McRae, an 'associate of thieves'. They were still at risk of being transported to Australia. Although the rate at which criminals were despatched Down Under was slowing, transportation did not stop until 1868.

GUILTY OR INNOCENT?

Constance Kent (left) was sentenced to death in 1865 for the murder, five years previously, of her four-year-old half-brother. The case was controversial. Kent had confessed to the killing, but many thought she was protecting her father, a known adulterer. Before she gave herself up, she had spoken to an Anglican clergyman who refused to repeat her statements to him in court on the grounds that she had made them under the seal of 'sacramental confession'. The Lord Chancellor ruled that under English law not even Roman Catholic clergy had the right to maintain the secrecy of the confessional in court, but no action was taken. The death sentence was commuted to imprisonment and Constance Kent served 20 years. After her release she emigrated to Tasmania where, after a blameless career as a nurse, she died aged 100.

NOT SO BEAUTIFUL

Sarah Rachel Leverson (below), known as Madam Rachel, ran a London beauty parlour catering for rich ladies, but her preparations were fakes. Her 'magnetic rock water dew' from the Sahara turned out to be water and bran. She also ran a sideline in procuring girls for the wealthy, then blackmailing the clients. She was eventually sentenced to 5 years for blackmail and died in prison.

The most notorious rookery was the 'Holy Land', which straddled New Oxford Street and Shaftesbury Avenue. It was easily reached by the lowlifes who preyed on passersby in the Haymarket and Regent Street. Once safely in, it was difficult for the police to winkle them out. The thieves had a rich slang all of their own: 'wires' picked ladies' pockets, 'thumble screwers' wrenched off watches, 'drag sneaks' stole from carts and coaches, 'drummers' drugged their victims' liquor, 'bluey hunters' stole lead from roofs, and 'snoozers' stayed at railway hotels looking for opportunities to make off with clothes and luggage.

Slowly, the worst of the rookeries were cleared from city centres. It took six years to build Holborn Viaduct, which saved horses the steep ascent from the Fleet Valley to the City. By the time it was completed in 1869, adorned with statues of Commerce, Agriculture, Science and Fine Art, thousands had been displaced from the slums that lined the Fleet River. The Law Courts – Victorian architecture at its most resplendent – were built on land recovered from the rookeries that had tarnished the top of Fleet Street.

CROWDED STREETS

Traffic was a growing problem in cities and especially in London, as this 1867 picture of a jam-packed London Bridge makes clear. Horse-drawn traffic was far less predictable and orderly than motor traffic, and there were frequent accidents. Pedestrians were often knocked down and injured – or worse.

London Bridge had been opened in 1831 (it was six years in the building, to a design by engineer John Rennie), but already it was congested and plans to widen it were being mooted. Widening took place in the early 20th century, but the extra weight proved too much and the bridge gradually began to sink. In 1968 a new London Bridge was opened and the old one was sold to an American oilman, who had it dismantled and shipped over to Arizona, where it was reassembled at Lake Havasu.

FAMILY PORTRAIT
A country family, not as large as most in an age when it was not unusual for a woman to have eight or ten children. The Victorians were fond of hunting, and gun dogs and shotguns were a natural part of country life. Field sports boomed, as industrialists bought sporting estates to prove themselves the equal of the old landed families. The watering can is indicative of another Victorian passion – gardening. In general, the 1860s were kind to the countryside, as farming boomed in the years before food imports from the Americas, Australasia and Denmark began to affect the home market in earnest.

to keep up to date, soon regaling readers with imperial dishes like Fricassee of Kangaroo Tail, or Parrot Pie – (1 doz. Paraqueets, 6 thin slices lean beef, 4 rashers bacon …) – and Quoorma Curry.

Moving out

Those who could afford to leave the smoke and stench of the cities moved outwards to new and leafy suburbs. The railways brought once dozy villages within commuting distance. Leeds had Headingley. Jesmond was the place of aspiration for the middle classes of Newcastle, as Edgbaston was for Birmingham. In London, Holland Park and Notting Hill were developed from the 1860s onwards. With tree-lined avenues, and garden squares, built in elegant white stucco, the huge houses would almost a century later become the rookeries of the 1950s before being regentrified.

Prosperous Victorian houses were cluttered with sideboards, bureaux, chiffoniers, pianos, dumbwaiters, revolving bookcases, prints, china, framed photographs, coal scuttles, gongs, waxed fruit, stuffed birds, vases, nursing chairs, club chairs, dining chairs, chintzes, display cases of butterflies, globes and figurines. The Victorians were great collectors of china figures, 'Staffordshires' for the most part, produced by scores of manufacturers in the Potteries. Royals, celebrities and statesmen were favourites. The top potter, W H Goss, covered the field from Queen Victoria to Disraeli and Lady Godiva. Animal figures sold in huge numbers, too, typically of cats and dogs, but also of more exotic creatures, like Jumbo, London Zoo's famous African elephant.

Country house building boomed as the new rich distanced themselves from the factories that spawned their wealth. A magnificent pile like Westonbirt, seven years in the building from 1863, set its owner back £125,000. A large town house might cost £2000 to build, a modest suburban villa £600.

continued on page 152

AFRICAN SUPERSTARS
Elephants were a popular zoo attraction. Jumbo the Elephant was bought by London Zoo in 1865 and became a star attraction, the biggest elephant in the zoo. There was a national outcry when he was sold to American showman Phineas T Barnum. Despite an attempted court injunction and a newspaper pledge to raise £100,000 to keep him in Britain, the 'biggest brute walking the Earth' was shipped to the New World, where he was killed three years later charging a railway train in Ontario.

BUILDING AND DESIGN

Mid-Victorian buildings – whether bridges or embankments, houses or hotels – were a reflection of the people who commissioned, designed and constructed them: finely detailed but solid, practical but exuberant, ultra-modern in technique but reliable – and supremely long-lasting.

BUILDING SUSPENDED
The Clifton Suspension Bridge over the Avon gorge is one of the world's most beautiful bridges. Its construction was also one of the most fraught.

The first competition to design the bridge, in 1829, was judged by Thomas Telford, the leading civil engineer of the day. Telford rejected all of the designs, proposed his own and was declared the winner. This result was so unpopular that a second competition was held, and this time was won by Isambard Kingdom Brunel, then just 24 years old. Despite his youth and inexperience, Brunel was appointed project engineer.

It was his first major commission and the project would outlast him. The foundation stone was laid in 1831, but the bridge soon ran into financial and political quicksands. In 1843 it was abandoned, with only the towers complete.

When Brunel died in 1859, it was realised that the bridge would be a fitting memorial. Work resumed – this photograph shows it underway in 1863 – and the bridge was at last opened the following year. Though Brunel designed it for the passage of light, horse-drawn traffic, it now carries 10,000 much heavier motor vehicles a day without complaint. The mid-Victorians built well, and to last.

A NEW RIVERSIDE

The Thames was the world's greatest waterway. It acquired its now familiar embankments in the 1860s as part of Bazalgette's sewage system for London. The river's extensive muddy banks were reclaimed and the river's edges built up to contain its waters and prevent flooding. This photograph (left) shows construction underway outside Somerset House in about 1865. When complete, the embankment concealed part of one of the main west-east sewers. It also provided space for a new road, public gardens and a station on the expanding Circle and District underground train service.

Further downriver the docks were growing apace. This is the view west from Trinity Wharf (bottom left). The terminal of the Blackwall Railway lies in the background on the right, while the forest of masts in the background on the left are ships in West India docks on the Isle of Dogs. The spoil from dock construction was taken up river and used to reclaim land. Battersea Park was one of the beneficiaries when its water meadows and market gardens were transformed into one of London's grandest parks

FIGURE HEADS

The stone lions were placed in Trafalgar Square around Nelson's Column in 1867. There was an imperial grandeur to the great beasts that reflected the growing empire. Trafalgar Square would eventually become the empire's heart, housing the offices of colonies and dominions. This was appropriate, because it was at the battle of Trafalgar that the Royal Navy established Britain's domination of the world's sealanes, thus making possible the whole extraordinary seaborne enterprise.

The recipes in a book of cottage cooking were for the likes of potato pie, stewed ox-cheek and mutton chitterlings. In Wiltshire, then a poor farming county, the Poor Law Commission found that bread, butter, potatoes, beer and tea were the staples. Only the skilled could afford bacon. The temptation to go poaching for fish and game made the gamekeeper and water bailiff ominous figures. They also ate 'slink', premature or stillborn calves, and 'broxy', diseased sheep.

The urban poor bought waste and offal from the butchers. A sheep's head sold for threepence. American bacon, at about sixpence a pound, was half the price of British bacon, but it was still beyond the reach of many. One in five of the silk workers in Macclesfield had never tasted meat.

Signs of satisfaction

Many, though, were able to save up for a day out. Victorian picnickers did not stint themselves. They drank Schweppes's Lemonade and Ginger Beer, and Masters' Pear Syrup, and ate their way through jellies, Bath buns, Banbury cakes, Victoria biscuits, hams, potted meats and sausage rolls. Furthermore, when out they behaved in a civilised manner that astonished Hippolyte Taine: 'I have seen

PARTY FEAST
The wedding of the Prince of Wales in 1863 was an excuse for national feasting. At St James's End in Northampton, an ox, a sheep, pig and hare were roasted in celebration. The meat was washed down with copious amounts of beer: ale was indeed safer to drink than water in an age when water supplies were often suspect.

whole families of the common people picnicking on the grass in Hyde Park,' the Frenchman wrote, 'and they neither pulled up nor damaged anything.'

Dinner was the midday meal for most people, though for the better-off it had become the evening meal. The writer R S Surtees described a dinner given for a master of foxhounds. It began with turtle soup, then moved on to 'turbot and lobster sauce ... mutton, turkey ... the game began to circulate ... grouse, woodcocks, partridges, snipes ... sweets in every sort of disguise – creams and jellies, and puffs and pastries – cream ice and water ice ... pineapple, grapes and Jersey pears ...'. This was washed down with some hock and white hermitage, then Moselle and a Burgundy, followed by port, Beaujolais, and bitter and sweet ales.

To be amply proportioned, in a man at least, was evidence of prosperity: his paunch was referred to as his 'corporation'. One banker – 'like most of my profession', he told *The Times*, 'I have my town-house in Belgravia and my villa at Roehampton' – who wrote to complain about traffic jams in the Strand admitted cheerfully that 'I am a fat man and am recommended horse exercise'. He was thrown when his horse shied at an advertising van. Fortunately, he said, 'being active though corpulent, I escaped unhurt'.

INDEX

PICTURE ACKNOWLEDGEMENTS

Abbreviations: t = top; m = middle; b = bottom; r = right; c = centre; l = left

All images in this book are courtesy of Getty Images, including the following which have additional attributions:
17, 31r, 73, 74, 119b, 152: Time & Life Pictures
25r, 34l, 54, 60, 156: Popperfoto
51, 125, 128, 130, 133: Sean Sexton
62: Museum of the City of New York
116l, 117: Julia Margaret Cameron/George Eastman House

LOOKING BACK AT BRITAIN
PEACE AND PROSPERITY – 1860s
is published by The Reader's Digest Association Ltd,
London, in association with Getty Images and
Endeavour London Ltd.

Copyright © 2009 The Reader's Digest Association Ltd

The Reader's Digest Association Ltd
11 Westferry Circus
Canary Wharf
London E14 4HE
www.readersdigest.co.uk

Endeavour London Ltd
21–31 Woodfield Road
London W9 2BA
info@endeavourlondon.com

Written by
Brian Moynahan

For Endeavour
Publisher: Charles Merullo
Designer: Tea Aganovic
Picture editor: Jennifer Jeffrey
Production: Mary Osborne

For Reader's Digest
Project editor: Christine Noble
Art editor: Conorde Clarke
Indexer: Marie Lorimer
Proofreader: Ron Pankhurst
Pre-press account manager: Dean Russell
Product production manager: Claudette Bramble
Production controller: Sandra Fuller

Reader's Digest General Books
Editorial director: Julian Browne
Art director: Anne-Marie Bulat

Colour origination by Chroma Graphics Ltd, Singapore
Printed and bound in Europe by Arvato Iberia

We are committed both to the quality of our
products and the service we provide to our customers.
We value your comments, so please do contact us on
08705 113366 or via our website at
www.readersdigest.co.uk

If you have any comments or suggestions about
the content of our books, email us at
gbeditorial@readersdigest.co.uk

CONCEPT CODE: UK 0154/L/S
BOOK CODE: 638-004 UP0000-2
ISBN: 978 0 276 44392 3
ORACLE CODE: 356900004H.00.24